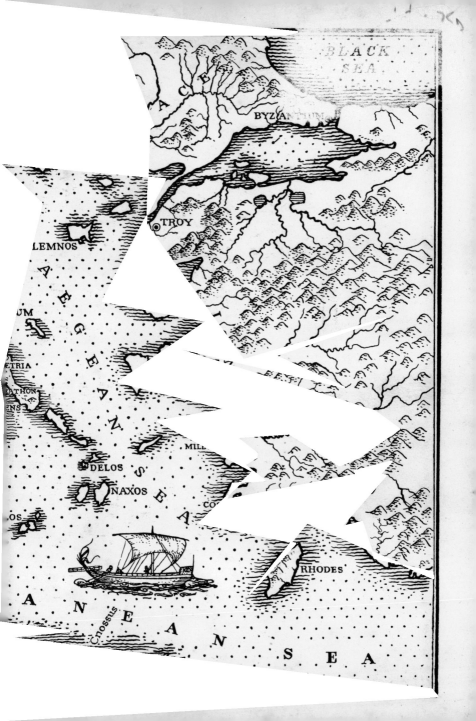

THE GREEKS AND THE ROMANS

IN TWO PARTS

PART I: THE GREEKS

The Greeks and the Romans

Part I

THE GREEKS

by

D. E. LIMEBEER, M.A.

Fellow of University College, London

Drawings and Maps by

E. A. McLAUGHLIN

CAMBRIDGE

at the University Press

1952

PUBLISHED BY
THE SYNDICS OF THE CAMBRIDGE UNIVERSITY PRESS

London Office: Bentley House, N.W.
American Branch: New York

Agents for Canada, India, and Pakistan: Macmillan

First Edition   1940
Second Edition 1952

First printed in Great Britain at The University Press, Cambridge
Reprinted by Spottiswoode, Ballantyne & Co., Ltd., Colchester

CONTENTS

ILLUSTRATIONS

PLATES

IN THE TEXT

MAPS AND PLANS

PREFACE TO FIRST EDITION

This book is mainly intended for part of a year's work in schools in ancient life and history. It can also be used concurrently with the ordinary classical course to supplement and integrate the pupils' reading of Greek authors. Experience shows that, if pupils are told everything, they remember little, and therefore an attempt has been made to stimulate their interest rather than to give them many relevant facts and details which could only become alive in a much longer book.

Chapters and sections on the literature have been given, together with translations of passages in prose and verse. The dates of the authors from whom quotations have been made have been given, but their value as historical evidence has not been stressed; the passages have been selected for their power of making the narrative vivid and memorable.

Accounts of the religion, art and social conditions have been included. Events, legends and expressions which have become part of our literature and thought have been given some prominence and, on wider issues, the debt of the modern world to Greece has been kept in mind.

In the spelling of Greek names and places, the general custom has been followed; even if this entails some inconsistency.

It is a pleasure to acknowledge with grateful thanks the help which has been given me by artists and authors or their relatives and publishers who have allowed me the use of copyright material. The source for the illustrations are shown in the list of plates and figures.

Permission has been given to use the translations of Homer by E. S. Barlow (the Shakespeare Head Press).

The translations of Plutarch have been taken partly from the version of A. H. Clough.

I owe special thanks to Professor T. B. L. Webster who read through the first draft of the manuscript and made many valuable suggestions. Without his help the book could hardly have been written. My thanks are also due to Miss A. M. Storeman, M.A. (formerly Headmistress of the Park School, Preston) for her suggestions and advice, and to Mr E. A. McClaughlin for the care and interest which he put into the illustrations and maps.

Finally, I must express my warm thanks to the Staff of the Cambridge University Press for all their patience, encouragement, and guidance in the making of the book.

D. E. LIMEBEER

December 1939

PREFACE TO SECOND EDITION. 1949

In addition to its use in schools, this book has also been found acceptable to adults as a first review of the subject, and as a background to their modern studies.

My thanks are due to Mrs T. B. L. Webster, M.A. (sometime Fellow of Lady Margaret Hall) for the valuable and unstinted help which she has given me in the revision of the book for a second edition.

D. E. LIMEBEER

July 1949

Part I
THE GREEKS

❦

INTRODUCTION

THE ANCIENT EMPIRES

This volume deals mainly with the history of Greece. Behind the story of Greece stretches a vast period in which civilization developed very slowly—a period at first shadowy, and then becoming more and more clear in the daylight of the facts of history.

Primitive man.

We know that for a very long stretch of the earth's history there were no men. Then we begin to find traces of primitive men who used simple tools, made for the most part of stone. This is called the Stone Age.[1] By degrees—so slowly that we, who live in an age of rapid discovery and invention, can hardly take in such slowness—these men learned a number of simple arts; they made and used a fire and a boat; they wove, and they made pottery; sowed crops and reared animals, to supply them with food, or with wool and skins for their clothes, or to carry them and their goods from one place to another. These stages we can discern dimly through the veil of time; only after many many years is the veil drawn aside so that we begin to see more clearly the lives and ways of men as they struggled towards civilization through the ages; some slowly, and others much more quickly.

[1] Part of the island of New Guinea is still in the Stone Age.

TIME CHART

Note. The ages before this do not concern our story except that
the Flood took place (date

Date	The Nile Valley	Mesopotamia	
4000–3000 B.C.		The Sumerians ,, ,, ,, ,, (Royal Tombs) ,, ,, Ur becomes less important Babylon becomes more important	
3000–2000 B.C.	Age of the Great Pyramids	Babylon ,, ,, ,, ,,	Assyria ,, ,, ,,
2000–1000 B.C.	The Hebrews in Egypt	,, ,,	,, ,,
1000–500 B.C.	Decline for a time in Egyptian power Babylon under Nebuchadnezzar	,, ,,	,, Fall of Assyria

THE GREAT RIVER VALLEYS

The people whose progress we can see most clearly lived in
the great river valleys, Mesopotamia and the Nile and the
Indus. Perhaps they had been driven there when the great
plains over which their ancestors wandered—such as the
Sahara or Arabia—had become desert land owing to change
in the climate of the earth. Let us see what we can find out

FROM 4000–500 B.C.

in Mesopotamia the settlement of the early Sumerians and unknown) before 4000 B.C.

THE HEBREWS	CRETE	GREECE	DATE
			4000–3000 B.C.
	Beginning of the Bronze Age in Crete		
			3000–2000 B.C.
Abraham			
			2000–1000 B.C.
	Cretan power at its height Fall of Cnossus		
The Exodus led by Moses Saul		Achaeans Dorians	
Israel conquered by Assyria Judah conquered by Babylon. The Exile		Formation of City-States of Greece	1000–500 B.C.

about the people who lived in two of these river valleys, Mesopotamia and the Nile.

Mesopotamia (the land 'between the rivers').

This region lies between two great rivers, the Euphrates and the Tigris, flowing through a wide plain, on which to-day many big mounds, or little hills, rise more or less steeply from the level ground. Many of the larger mounds, or groups of them, contain cities which were burnt or raided or otherwise destroyed in the far past, and then collapsed, each on top of the one before, making a mound like cake in layers. Many of these have been excavated; that is to say, the ground has been dug out and has revealed quantities of objects which show the life and civilization of the inhabitants.

Map 1. The Eastern Empires.

The Sumerians.

One of these excavations was carried out at Ur, a city of an ancient people called the Sumerians, who lived in the southern part of Mesopotamia. Now the people of Ur had an untidy habit of throwing their rubbish (fragments of pottery and so on) over the city walls, and this has been dug out by excavators. Below it, however, they came to a layer of clay, eight feet deep, which contained no traces of man or his handiwork, and the excavators realized that the clay must have been deposited by a great river flood round Ur, in the midst of which the city stood up like an island, and that this was the Flood mentioned in the Bible, for that story came from Mesopotamia and describes an event which really happened. The waters covered a very wide expanse; it is no wonder that the story was handed down that they had covered the whole earth. Below the clay, fragments were found dating from before the flood. Outside the city *above* the flood area, and therefore later in date, the excavators found, deep down, the royal tombs, of which the earliest date from soon after 3500 B.C., containing traces of a rich civilization; the bodies in the tombs were adorned with wreaths and ornaments of beautifully wrought gold; a dagger was found there, a gold helmet, and parts of harps ornamented with gold and with blue stones, all hidden from sight for about 5000 years.

Another stretch of centuries, and a still higher layer of the ruined city brings us to the period of a very real person of world history whose name was Abraham; he seems quite modern compared with the more distant period which we have just described. In his time (about 2100 B.C.) Ur was a prosperous city of craftsmen and merchants, who traded far and wide by river or caravan routes and made records of their business transactions on clay tablets on which were 'written' words, made by pressing a little instrument into the clay while it was still damp. Many of these clay tablets are in our museums to-day. The houses of Ur were often comfortable and spacious, sometimes with ten or twelve rooms, a private chapel, and an inner balcony over a central hall in which were braziers filled with charcoal for warmth and great jars of water brought from well or river by slaves.

Such was the civilization which Abraham knew when, as the Bible tells us, he left Ur (and its worship of many gods) with his family, 'not knowing whither he went,' and found at last a home in Canaan. He had turned his back on Ur, but he carried with him into his new life a knowledge of a civilization far greater than that of the people among whom he was now to dwell. We will now leave Mesopotamia for a time and look at the civilization of the river valley of the Nile.

THE NILE

Evidently people lived in this valley for many generations of the Stone Age, for in the earliest tombs stone tools are found by the side of the bodies of the buried men. The Nile itself led the inhabitants on to further knowledge and skill, since, by its regular rise and fall, it made the land fertile and trade possible. The men were forced to irrigate their lands and keep constant moisture in their fields; thus their need for inventions grew, and with their need their skill grew too, so that quite early in the history of Egypt (perhaps about 4000 B.C.) the use of *metals* for tools and implements was discovered, which in its turn led on to still greater needs and achievements.

We will pass quickly over more than 2000 years to the time when (as we read in Genesis) a stranger (Joseph), came from Palestine to Egypt, and saw around him the works of an advanced civilization—the great stone Pyramids (which were already over 1000 years old), the magnificent temples, the figures carved in wood and stone, and the rich clothes and jewellery of the Egyptians. He did not yet know that one day, in time of famine, he was to be the adviser of the Pharaoh (King) and to control the stores of grain saved from the teeming cornlands of the Nile.

Some centuries after the time of Joseph, the Children of Israel, who had settled in Egypt, were led back to Palestine by Moses, and Egypt remained for a long time not only powerful within her own boundaries, but able to threaten or assist the little country of Palestine in which the Children of Israel lived. Then after another 500 years a change came, and we find a great prophet of Israel, called Isaiah, warning his people not to 'strengthen themselves with the strength of Pharaoh, or trust in the shadow of Egypt'; for Egypt had lost much of her power and could not protect them against the new enemy which was threatening them both from Mesopotamia, to which country we will now return.

The Semites.

By this time Sumeria had been conquered by some invaders from the north, called Semites, one branch of whom settled on the Euphrates, and later founded Babylon; another branch, the Assyrians, settled on the Tigris. The Babylonians and the Assyrians often fought each other, and both tried to conquer Palestine and Egypt. Here again we touch Bible history at point after point, leading up to the moment when the mighty King Nebuchadnezzar took Jerusalem (586 B.C.) and carried off the inhabitants to his great city, Babylon.

We shall hear in Chapter VI how later the Jews returned to Jerusalem. They had been in Babylon for over fifty years, and many of them had been born there. When they left they took with them some of the knowledge and civilized ways of the East. Moreover, trading was now going on everywhere in the ancient world, carrying with it from country to country not only merchandise but ideas, and in this way also the world progressed.

Long before this a great civilization had sprung up in the Mediterranean. Its centre was Crete, but it owed much to its contact with the Eastern and Egyptian cultures which we have just described. The Cretan, or as it is usually called the Minoan, civilization flourished from before 3000 to 1400 B.C., and then it gave way to the civilization of Greece, which is the subject of this book.

THE KINGS OF CRETE

All history begins with myths or stories, which are so full of strange and marvellous things that they seem like fairy tales. Still, there is always some truth in them and much real history, if we only dig deep enough.

Here is a story of Crete, an island in the Aegean Sea, and of its famous king, Minos.

Minos was the son of Zeus, greatest of all the gods. He became a powerful king, and was not only ruler over his own island, Crete, but was, in effect, lord of the Aegean. His son had been treacherously slain in Athens, and in revenge he forced the king to send him every ninth year a tribute of seven youths and seven maidens. These were to be sacrificed to the Minotaur—a great bull-headed monster kept by the king in the labyrinth which had been made for him by his craftsman, Daedalus. Twice the ship from Athens brought across the Aegean its freight of youths and maidens; twice they were taken into the labyrinth and killed. The third time Theseus, the son of Aegeus, king of Athens, determined to go himself to Crete, and there to slay the monster and put an end to this shame of Athens. He was brought before Minos, who put him into prison to await his doom. However, Ariadne, the king's daughter, who had fallen in love with Theseus, went secretly to the prison and gave him a sword with which to kill the monster, and a ball of thread to guide him back again out of the windings of the labyrinth. Theseus slew the Minotaur, found his way out by means of the clue, freed his companions and then, with them and Ariadne, sailed away from Crete.

He had promised his father, Aegeus, that his sailors would

hoist a black sail if he had been destroyed, and a white one if he was still alive. Unfortunately, this order was forgotten, and Aegeus, seeing the black-sailed ship approach Athens and not doubting that the worst had happened, threw himself into the sea, and that is why that part of the Mediterranean is called the Aegean.

Fig. 1. Cnossus; the throne room (restored)

This is the tale of the labyrinth, its monster and its unhappy offering of youths and maidens.

It has now been discovered that the island kingdom of Crete was for a long time all-powerful in the Aegean, and that its chief city was Cnossus.[1] The Greeks believed that there was a king called Minos, and it is thought that he (or a line of kings bearing this name) may have reigned during a time of high prosperity in Cretan history. His power was so great that foreign cities paid him tribute, and the civilization of

[1] This is the Latin spelling. The Greek was Knossos.

the Bronze Age in which he lived is called Minoan. We can follow the details of the life and state of Minos and other great kings of Crete, because, since the beginning of this century, archaeologists, starting from the late Sir Arthur Evans, have dug so far into the soil that they can give us an account of its civilization from about 3000 B.C. or earlier. All the things mentioned in this chapter have been discovered—either themselves or pictures of them—below the soil of Crete.

We can imagine one of these kings in his palace at Cnossus, rich, stern and far-seeing, sitting on his high-backed throne among his counsellors, ordering his realm and dispensing justice. He had his pastimes, too. He loved to watch the famous bull-leaping contests in some open space near the palace. Face to face with the huge animal stood the brave gymnast (one of the young men or women trained for this task). The bull charged with lowered head; the gymnast dodged it, seized a horn, swung himself over the creature's head, and for a moment grazed it or even lay on it back to back. Then with a somersault he landed clear behind the bull, where another gymnast was waiting to catch him.

One part of the palace at Cnossus consisted of a great flagged court, with room for four or five hundred spectators, overlooked by a wide flight of steps and by the royal 'box', high above it at

Fig. 2. Woman in Minoan dress.

the back. Here took place contests in wrestling, boxing, and ball games, and above all, the famous dances of Cretan youths and maidens accompanied by the music of the lyre and pipe. Among the spectators were the Cretan ladies, elaborately dressed in long, flounced skirts with tight waists and their hair in ringlets.

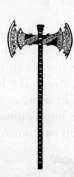

Fig. 3. The double axe. (There is also a simpler form with one plain blade on each side.)

Fig. 4. A Cretan jar.

The whole palace covered five acres and was in some places three or four storeys high. This palace or its ruins may possibly have given rise to the Greek story of the labyrinth—a word which came later to mean a maze with complicated passages from which people could not easily find their way without guidance. The word 'labyrinth' may originally have meant 'the place of the axes', and have been derived from 'labrys', which means a double-headed axe—a symbol used by the Cretans, engraved on pillars and elsewhere in the palace.

As for the bull—in many parts of the island objects and pictures have been found, which seem to show that the bull was a sacred animal in Crete.

We are beginning to see traces of history behind the story of the Minotaur and the labyrinth.

The great king had other interests than sport. He had, in part of his palace at Cnossus, potter's workshops in which were made the famous Cretan vases with their lovely patterns and bright colours. His storerooms were full of jars which were made in his pottery and were large enough to contain a man (like those in the story of Ali Baba and the Forty Thieves). These jars held immense quantities of wine, oil and grain for the use of the king and his soldiers, his officials, his artists, sculptors and armour-makers, his attendants, and any foreigners that came to his court.

Crete was a lovely island, with its mountains, harbours, and its trees and flowers (such as irises, roses and crocuses). In it were ninety cities and multitudes of people, some busy with the weaving and dyeing of cloth or the making of gold ornaments and bronze inlaid armour, some going to sea in ships, some hunting, or ploughing and sowing the fields.

Far and wide trading went on between Crete and the lands within its reach. Copper came from Cyprus and tin possibly

Fig. 5. The cupbearer (painted on the wall in reddish colour).

from Cornwall. Amber may have crossed Europe from the Baltic to the Black Sea and thence by the Aegean Sea to Crete; such things as stone vessels, ivory and beads came from Egypt, while Crete in return sent out quantities of oil and wine and works of art, and the metal work for which it was famous.

This exchange of goods was easy, for Crete had conquered or sent settlers to many places in the Aegean and beyond it, and not even the great independent powers like Egypt were likely to refuse traffic with the 'Lord of the Aegean' when he sent his ships sailing over the 'liquid roads' of the sea. Pirates were kept down by him with a stern hand.

The kings had not even fortified their cities, for they trusted to the fear of their name, their navy and the protecting sea, to keep safe their proud and wealthy kingdom, but another danger had more than once assailed it. Crete was subject to earthquakes which overthrew its palaces, but these were rebuilt each time with more magnificence than before.

In about 1400 B.C. the island suffered from a catastrophe which was so sudden that, in Cnossus, the sacred oil stood ready to pour into vases for a religious ceremony, which never took place, and in other parts of the island there were proofs of an unexpected disaster which cut men off in the midst of their work. Fire raged and destroyed. It is now thought that this was caused by an earthquake, though enemies may have added to the destruction.

There was some rebuilding at Crete, but the life of the city never fully recovered. The sea-power of the island seems to have continued for a time, but gradually its navy weakened and pirates once more roamed the sea.

Its culture and influence had already been stamped on the mainland of Greece, and so its civilization did not die. Our own knowledge of this civilization is due to the spade, and not to the written word, for though scholars can read the Cretan alphabet, they cannot understand its language. This is like a closed door between us and a detailed knowledge of the history of Crete. Perhaps one day someone will unlock it.

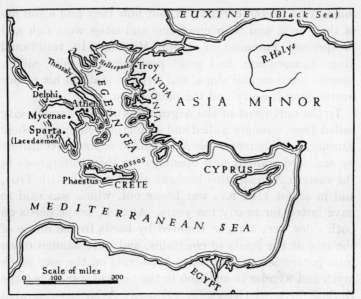

Map 2. The Eastern Mediterranean.

II

HOMER AND THE HEROIC AGE

GREECE AND TROY

Our scene now shifts to the mainland of Greece. Here, at one time, Crete had had great power, but even before its fall people of the race called Achaean had been moving south- wards from their homes in the northern part of Greece, and had become so powerful that by about 1200 B.C. they were the strongest people on the Aegean Sea. They had learnt

Note. The civilization of this age, including that of the cities Mycenae and Troy, was revealed by the German excavator Schliemann in the last quarter of the nineteenth century.

much from Cretan civilization, but now they had a full life of their own, and their chieftains and cities were rich and prosperous. Foremost of all was Mycenae. Its traditional king, Agamemnon, had great possessions of gold, silver, bronze, chariots and ships, and lived in state in his palace overlooking the city and the plain below.

To the north-east of the Aegean was another famous city called Troy, strongly walled and set on the Hellespont, where Europe and Asia meet. The Achaeans were bold adventurers by sea, and wanted new openings for their enterprises in the eastern Aegean; this brought about a clash with Troy, and in about 1190 B.C. war broke out, which was said to have lasted for nearly ten years. After it, brave deeds on both sides were sung or chanted by bards to the music of the lyre at the feasts of chieftains, and were handed down from generation to generation, gathering on the way much myth and wonder in addition to the facts of war. When the Dorians invaded Greece (p. 25) many Achaeans migrated from Greece to Ionia on the coast of Asia Minor, and brought across with them these stories, which were thus kept alive and made into long poems by poets, of whom far the greatest was Homer. He is supposed to have been blind and to have lived in Ionia in about 900 B.C. Seven places in this region claimed to be his birthplace. We really know very little about him except that he was one of the greatest of all poets. He produced two epics,[1] the *Iliad*[2] (which tells of part of the war at Troy) and the *Odyssey* (which tells of the adventures of Odysseus on his return to Greece).

The story on which he worked was this: Paris, son of Priam, king of Troy, carried off Helen, the beautiful wife of Menelaus, king of Sparta, brother of Agamemnon. Though

---

[1] Homer did not actually compose the whole of these epics but worked into one whole his own poems and those of other poets.
[2] Ilion is another name for Troy.

Helen had gone willingly, the Greek cities, under the leadership of Agamemnon, joined in an expedition against Troy which ended in the destruction of the city. The Trojans were killed in war or carried off as captives and only a few remained among the ruins of their city. The Greeks returned victorious to their homes.

In the story as told by Homer, the gods and goddesses of the Greeks take their part. These will be explained in Chapter IV and in the Appendix; the only ones that concern us here are Zeus (the greatest of the gods); Apollo, god of music, poetry and prophecy; Pallas Athene, goddess of wisdom; Hermes, messenger of the gods; and Hephaestus, god of the arts which are worked by fire.

Fig. 6. Harnessing a chariot (from a black figured vase).

THE *ILIAD*

When the poem opens, Achilles, the greatest hero on the Greek side, is seen in his tent, resentful and brooding because his war-captive, the maiden Briseis, had been assigned to Agamemnon. This was his reward—cried Achilles—for long days and nights of watching, for fighting,

and capturing cities and treasures, all handed over to
Agamemnon as his overlord.

And so 'he betook himself neither to the place of
gathering...nor to war, but consumed his own heart in
tarrying in his place, and longed for the war-cry and for
battle'.

Meanwhile, courageous deeds without number were done on
both sides. The gods took this side or that, and Zeus held the
golden scales weighing the destinies of Greeks and Trojans.

The bravest warrior on the side of Troy was Hector, son
of King Priam. He bade farewell to his wife and little son
on the city battlements; he could not listen to her entreaties
that he would stay.

> Then bronze-helmed Hector answered her once more:
> 'Dear wife, there is much wisdom in your words.
> Yet if I shrink I shall be shamed before
> the long-robed Trojan women and their lords.
> Nay further, my own soul no place affords
> for cowardice. My task, to stand alone
> and wield the foremost of the Trojan swords,
> winning my father's glory and my own.
> Yet in my inmost heart and soul one thing is known.'

He stretched out his arms to the child, who, frightened
at the nodding crest of his helmet, shrank back into his
nurse's arms. So—laying his helmet aside—Hector took
up the child and prayed to Zeus that he should be valiant
and victorious, greater than himself.

> Then laughed his father and his mother mild
> and Hector laid the helmet on the ground
> all gleaming bright. He took and kissed his child,
> praying to Zeus and all the gods around:
> 'Grant, Zeus, that this my son be valiant found
> even as I; may his renown shine bright
> among the Trojans, and his strength abound.
> Then men shall say "He doth surpass in might
> his father", when he comes back, victor in the fight.'

Then he went out against the foe, knowing in his heart and soul that he himself would be killed, and that Troy would fall.

He slew many enemies; he even leapt over the wall of the Greek camp, called to his men to follow him, and scattered the Greeks in flight. Next he killed Patroclus, Achilles' greatest friend, and finally the two, Achilles, fired to vengeance, and Hector met in single combat.

Achilles' armour had been made for him by the god Hephaestus, and his shield was the most famous in literature, for it was wrought of gold, silver and bronze, and on it were engraved many scenes of the life of the day—a marriage festival, a dispute in the market-place, armies at siege, a vineyard, a harvest, plough-land and pasture.

> And then a dancing place he fashioned there
> such as once Daedalus in Cnossus made,
> that wide spread city, for a lady fair,
> the maiden Ariadne of the lovely hair.

> And there were young men dancing on that ground
> and girls much courted, hardly to be won;
> hand holding wrist, they trod the measure round.
> The girls wore linen fine, the youths had on
> tunics all woven fair that faintly shone
> with oil. A wreath adorned each maiden's head.
> The youths bore daggers wrought of gold alone
> from silver baldrics hanging. Thus they sped
> with deft feet circling round, and lightly did they tread.

> Just so a potter by his wheel doth sit,
> that fits between his hands, and for a test
> whether it duly runs, so turns he it.
> Then back in ordered lines each met the rest.
> There round the lovely band stood many a guest,
> for whom the godlike minstrel raised a strain
> of lyric song, and gladness filled their breast.
> And through them all there circled tumblers twain
> to lead the measure, passing through the midst again.

Achilles attacked Hector, who at last fled before him. Then, like Ares, god of war— like a falcon after a dove, like a hound after a fawn, Achilles followed him. Zeus held the golden scales and Hector's fate sank down.

> Fierce rage Achilles then did overwhelm
> so as he rushed, holding before his breast
> his graven shield, and tossed his shining helm
> round which there waved four golden plumes as crest
> there by Hephaestus set. So, loveliest
> of all the stars in heaven doth Hesperus go
> on a dark night outshining all the rest.
> Thus in Achilles' right hand, even so
> Flashed his keen spear as he devised his deadly blow.

The blow fell and Hector, dying, begged Achilles to give his body burial and warned him that he too would meet his fate under the walls of Troy.

> Then bright-helmed Hector dying spake once more:
> 'Truly I know you well and plainly see
> your heart is iron hard, immovable by me.
>
> Yet you by Paris and Apollo slain
> shall surely perish at the Scaean gate
> for all your might. Take heed then once again
> lest I should draw on you God's bitter hate.'
> He ended, and bewailing his sad fate
> his soul sped forth and must to Hades wend,
> stripped of her youth and vigour desolate.

Without answering Hector's plea for burial, and taking no thought for his own fate, Achilles killed him with his spear.

> Then great Achilles spake: 'Make now an end,
> and I too will accept what doom the gods may send.'

Priam, the aged king, came as a suppliant for his son's body, and Achilles, moved to pity, gave it to him for burial.

Here the *Iliad* ends, for its subject is 'the wrath of Achilles', which began with his quarrel with Agamemnon and ended with the burial of the man who killed his greatest friend.

THE *ODYSSEY*

This poem tells us how, after ten long years of wandering, Odysseus, a Greek chieftain, reached his island home of Ithaca.

Here Penelope, wife of Odysseus, had for three years been weaving a web and secretly unravelling it night by night, for she was beset by many suitors who would force her to choose between them when the work was finished. These suitors came daily to her house with insolent pride; they sacrificed oxen, sheep and goats, and drank her wine recklessly, wasting the wealth of the house. At last her secret was betrayed by one of her women, but help now came to her from Olympus, the abode of the gods, whence Pallas Athene, 'swift as the breath of the wind, sped over the sea and over the boundless earth to her aid'. Telemachus, the young son of Odysseus, inspired by her, defied the suitors.

> 'Waste your own substance, going from house to house
> in turn. Yet if it seem a better thing
> to eat up one man's substance and carouse
> all unrequited, on with revelling.
> Yet will I pray the deathless gods to bring
> vengeance, that Zeus due recompense may send
> and you all unrequited meet your end.'

Telemachus had suddenly shown himself a man and lord of his house. All were amazed and the suitors lay in wait to kill him.

Meanwhile, Odysseus was nearing the end of his adventures. For seven years the goddess Calypso had kept him in her

lovely isle, 'trying to win him with her guileful words to
forgetfulness of Ithaca', but he was eating his heart out
with longing for home. At last Zeus sent the god Hermes
to release him.

> Over Pieria passing speedily
> back from the upper air swift Hermes sped
> and dipped down like a cormorant to the sea
> that hunting, chases fish across the dread
> gulfs of the mighty deep unharvested.
> All his thick plumage in the brine he laves.
> Thus Hermes rode upon the thronging waves.

Hermes delivered his message, and Odysseus was allowed
to make a raft and set out. After seventeen days he
sighted an island, like a shield in the misty sea: it was the
land of the Phaeacians but, before he reached that kindly
isle, a great storm wrecked his raft and he swam for two days
and nights till he saw a land of jutting headlands, cliffs,
and reefs, with roaring surging waves. Washed to shore by a
great wave, he swam up a river mouth, and landed safely on
the bank.

Meanwhile, Nausicaa, daughter of King Alcinous, had
come with her maidens to wash her clothes 'in the lovely
stream of the river, with its pools and welling springs'.

> Then from the waggon in their hands they bore
> the garments forth, and took them down amain,
> there in the troughs by the dark water's shore
> in busy rivalry. When every stain
> was cleared away, they spread them out again
> along the sea shore, where the breakers most
> wash clean the pebbles, beating on the coast.

> And when they'd bathed and were with olive oil
> anointed well, they picnicked and did lie
> beside the river's banks at rest from toil,
> waiting until the sun's bright beams should dry

> the washing. Then they laid their wimples by
> after the meal, and started to play ball,
> the king's fair daughter and the maidens all.

The last ball missed its mark, and fell in the river, waking Odysseus, who was in a deep sleep. Then, at the bidding of Nausicaa, he went to the beautiful palace of Alcinous, where he was most hospitably entertained. He told them his adventures—how he escaped from the Cyclops, a one-eyed giant, from a raging storm, from the enchantress Circe and the beguiling Sirens, and from the peril of passing between the sea-monsters, Scylla and Charybdis. The next day Alcinous set him in one of his magic ships 'swift as a bird in flight or a thought', and he was borne to Ithaca. Though disguised as an old beggar-man, he was recognized by his aged nurse, and by his dog Argos—once so swift a runner, so brave a hunter, and now old, feeble and neglected. He lifted his head and pricked his ears, and then

> He wagged his tail and both his ears laid low,
> yet to his master had no strength to go.
>
> And when he saw Odysseus in that hour
> of meeting, now that twenty years were past,
> then black death fell on Argos at the last.

With the help of Telemachus, who now knew the truth, Odysseus slew the suitors with his mighty bow, and then revealed himself to Penelope.

The havoc and the din of fighting were over, and all was quiet in the shadowy halls.

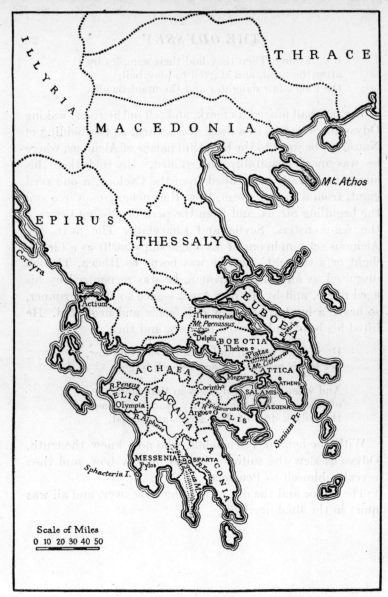

Map 3. Greece.

(The peninsula from Achaea and Corinth to the south coast
is called the Peloponnese.)

III

MOVEMENTS BY LAND AND SEA
from about 1100 B.C.

THE DORIAN INVASION

The Achaeans were not long left in peace, for invaders from the North and North-west called Dorians poured into Greece destroying and conquering. These invasions took place at about the time of transition from the Bronze to the Iron age. The Dorians used iron, (now commonly mined), for weapons as well as for tools, and could now arm the mass of their fighters as heavy infantry, thus winning an easier victory over the Achaeans.

The Dorians occupied Corinth and nearly all of the Peloponnese. They took some of the towns and destroyed others, including Mycenae; Sparta became a Dorian city. Athens, which was off their main route, was left untouched, and many of the Achaeans, driven from their homes, settled in Attica (the district round Athens) and the island of Euboea. When these places became overcrowded, they migrated to the coast of Asia Minor. Their settlements became the rich, prosperous and cultured Ionian cities of which we shall hear much in these pages.

We thus have Achaeans and Dorians in mainland Greece, both speaking Greek though in somewhat different dialects, and another group of Greek-speaking people on the other side of the Aegean.

THE GROWTH OF THE CITY STATES

The story of Greece for two hundred years or so after the coming of the Dorians is vague and confused, but gradually it becomes clearer to us. By about 800 B.C. a number of cities, each with its own life and government, had begun to develop. The mountains and inlets of Greece gave to each of them natural barriers against outsiders, and, though they used the same language, they were quite independent of one another, and often quarrelled among themselves. These city-states, as they are called, included a certain amount of the country round. Many of the Aegean islands were small enough to form single city-states.

COLONIZATION[1]

As the cities grew, the boundaries of their states became too narrow for the population, and many citizens had to look elsewhere for lands to settle in. Often they were discontented at home, especially the workers on the land, who led a life of hard and grinding toil; often they were men of adventurous spirit, eager to open up new centres of trade. For these reasons colonists went out in all directions and settled round the seas like 'frogs round a pond'.

There were still pirates at sea, and some of the early colonists were pirates themselves. For example, one set of colonists settled in the Lipari islands near Sicily, and here half of them worked the land, while the other half lay in watch for the rich Etruscan ships from Italy, and plundered them. In time, however, the Greek cities put a stop to this barbarous custom, and organized their colonization in the following way.

First, the oracle at Delphi was consulted to see if the gods favoured the enterprise. Then a leader was chosen, and ships were prepared—usually long, swift sailing ships with fifty oars. Their way across the Aegean was easy, for they were seldom out of sight of the islands which guided them like

---

[1] The greatest period for this was from 770 to 650 B.C.

Sparta had already conquered Laconia and had seized its best lands. The inhabitants who submitted remained free and supported themselves by manufacture and by trade at home and abroad, but were not counted as Spartan citizens; they were called Perioikoi ('the dwellers round'). Those who resisted to the end became serfs and were called Helots. Later on the Spartans crossed the mountain ridge of Taygetus to the west, and invaded the fertile lands of Messenia. The inhabitants fought bravely and stubbornly, but at last their strongholds were stormed; they had to submit and become Helots.

All these Helots had portions of land allotted to them where they were obliged to live and work, paying their masters a fixed amount of their produce. They had to serve them in war, but in times of peace they were forbidden to move away from their land, which was allotted to them. Still, they were not exactly slaves, for they could not be sold and some of them became quite well off when their farms prospered. They soon outnumbered the Spartans, who were in constant fear that this proud, conquered race would rise up against them, and they even had a kind of secret police who moved about among the Helots and killed those whom they suspected. The Spartans knew that this cruel practice was not enough; they must strengthen *themselves* in every possible way, and so they suppressed all luxury, kept out foreign trade by having only an iron coinage, expelled foreigners when they found it convenient, and made themselves into a nation of soldiers. 'Their city', says Plutarch,[1] 'was a sort of armed camp, in which every man had his share of provisions and business set out, and looked on himself as born to serve his country.'

From birth, the life of a true-born Spartan belonged to

[1] Born about 46 A.D.; a Greek, whose writings are interesting and vivid, but not always historically reliable.

the state. Only strong and healthy babies were allowed to live; the weak ones were carried to Mt Taygetus and left there to die.

At the age of seven, boys were taken from home and were trained by the state until they were twenty. They learned reading, writing, music, some arithmetic, and passages from Homer or from their own poet Tyrtaeus. No literature was allowed that was not warlike, nor any practice in elegant speech or writing, for the Spartans despised words and used so few of them in their talk that the word 'laconic' (from 'Laconia') is used even now for a bare, curt way of speaking. Running, wrestling and quoit-throwing made the boys strong and agile, and their other training made them hardy and brave and fit to become leaders when the time came.

They wore only one garment, and they went barefoot; they slept on rushes which they had gathered by the river, adding some thistledown in winter, and they had only plain and meagre food which they eked out by stealing. If caught, they were whipped, not for stealing, but for 'thieving so awkwardly'. They were whipped once a year to accustom them to endure pain. From eighteen to twenty they had special training in warfare, and from twenty to thirty they became instructors of the younger boys and were allowed to marry but not to live at home. From thirty onwards they became full citizens (called 'equals') and lived at their homes, but they still had their main meals in barracks, and were not allowed to leave the city without permission, in case of a call to arms.

Fifteen men shared a table at their meals. If any man wanted to join one of these groups each of the fourteen others took a ball of soft bread (his 'voting paper') and dropped it into a basin. If a ball had been flattened, the new comer was not admitted, for it showed that at least one member did not want him. Each man supplied his share of barley meal, wine, cheese and figs, and some money to buy fish and meat. They were all dressed alike in a garment dyed in purple, and were close comrades in peace and war. Together they marched out to battle to the sound of the flute.

Fig. 11. A heavy-armed Greek warrior.

Spartan girls were trained in mind and body to become brave mothers of brave men. They practised athletic exercises like the boys, and when they married, they urged their men to deeds of valour. A Spartan mother is said to have told her son to return from battle either with his great shield or on it—for no soldier would cast away his shield except in flight; better to be borne home on it dead.

The Government.

Sparta had two kings at the same time, who gradually lost most of their power. The work was then done by the five Ephors ('overseers') and a council of twenty-eight elders who, with the Ephors, were so powerful that they could even summon the kings before them.

The people in their Assembly met at least once a month to vote on measures proposed by the Council, but they were not allowed to discuss them, and sometimes the Council seems to have taken no notice of the way that they had voted.

Lycurgus.

The Spartans themselves came to believe that all the arrangements had been made for them by a lawgiver called Lycurgus, a wise man who wanted to help his city and did not aim at power for himself. When he had finished his work, he left the country, having first made the Spartans promise to keep his laws till he came back. He went at once to the oracle at Delphi, which told him that Sparta would prosper so long as she kept his laws; he therefore never returned to Sparta and was never heard of again. Such was the story, but the dates are too vague and the figure of Lycurgus is too shadowy for us to accept it as real history.

But it is true without doubt that Sparta had—and kept— the extraordinary rules and regulations described in this chapter, and that she became the strongest military power by land in Greece.

ATHENS

Sparta was like no other Greek city, but Athens was typical of many Greek cities, though she far outshone them all. Sparta was bound by rigid, unchanging laws—an oligarchy governed by a few men—but Athens became a free and noble state—a democracy governed by her citizens in accordance with the people's will. We shall see in this chapter how she achieved this, step by step.

Athens and Attica.

Whereas Sparta conquered Laconia and Messenia by force and held them by fear, Athens held Attica by its own

Fig. 12. Olive gatherers (from a black figured vase).

consent, for, early in Athenian history, the small towns of Attica came, mainly by peaceable arrangement, under her protection as part of her city-state. This was fortunate for Athens, since it surrounded her with friends and gave her a large territory (1000 square miles) containing some natural resources—marble and stone in her mountains, silver and lead in her mines, clay in her rivers for her pottery, olives and vines in plenty, and some corn, but not enough as her numbers grew. On the land side Attica was sheltered by mountains, but not hemmed in, as there were passes across them which could be used in friendly times. The coast, jutting out towards the Aegean islands and the east, seemed to point the way to adventure by sea, and quite soon many ships sailed out from its harbours, laden with olive oil and pottery to be exchanged for corn, so that there was busy trafficking on the Aegean.

At first Athens was ruled by kings, but in about 650 B.C. a change was made, not by revolution but peaceably. The kings, who had gradually lost their power, now ceased to rule even in name, and the government of the state was in the hands of a few noble families, led by magistrates called archons,[1] chosen from their number. The people were divided into classes according to their wealth, and all classes except the lowest voted in the Assembly of the People. Here they may have sanctioned formally the election of the archons, who on taking office swore to rule according to the laws and not to take any bribe. If they failed in this, they were to dedicate at Delphi a golden statue (possibly of life-size.)

Soon there were difficulties, especially among the poorest class, which had no rights, and so, for the next one hundred and fifty years, changes were made from time to time, leading Athens towards democracy.

Draco.

In 621 B.C. an archon called Draco was asked to draw up a list of the laws of Athens. Draco and his code of laws are only vaguely known to us, but it seems clear that the punishments inflicted were very harsh, and even to-day such laws are often called Draconian. Plutarch tells us that death was the penalty for nearly all offences—for stealing an apple or a cabbage, for idleness, or for murder. He wrote at least 700 years after Draco's time and his statement may

---

[1] Three at first, but later on, nine elected annually.

or may not be accurate, but there is no doubt that the Greeks themselves thought the laws very severe, and agreed with the Athenian orator who said that they were written, not in ink but in blood. Still, it was a real step forward for the Athenians to have the laws by which they were governed set out in writing for all to see. These laws were soon replaced by much better ones.

Solon.

We have now passed the age of shadowy figures like Lycurgus and of little-known ones like Draco, and we have come to the first really historical figure in Greek history.

Solon belonged to a noble Athenian family and was a rich merchant who, in his travels, had noticed how other cities were governed. He resolved to help Athens and 'to do some high thing for his country'. In 594 B.C. he was elected archon.

Now in Attica there were many small farmers who were so poor that they had to borrow money at high interest from the big landowners and other rich men on the security of their land. This means that they mortgaged their lands, i.e. that they undertook to give them up to their creditors if they could not pay their debts. These lands were marked by boundary stones (sometimes called mortgage pillars) and often they stood there unmoved if the debtor failed to pay. He continued working on land that had once been his own and seems to have paid one-sixth of its produce to his creditor. Sometimes men who had no land, or could not produce their quota, had to pledge both themselves and their families, and when the debt still remained unpaid, they were in the position of slaves who could be sold at home or overseas by their masters.

Solon (to use his own words) 'pulled up the boundary stones'. He freed the slaves, forbade men to sell themselves, and cancelled debts thus incurred. This was called by a Greek word which means 'the shaking off of burdens', and they saved Athens from having all round her men who would have been as ill-treated, as miserable and as dangerous as the Helots were all through Spartan history.

Solon tried to make the Athenians good and public-spirited citizens. He divided the people into classes, and gave even the lowest class, the labourers, the right to vote at the Assembly of the People; he set up law courts with citizens as jurymen; he welcomed foreigners to Athens, encouraged trade, and insisted on accurate weights and measures. No one was to speak ill of the living in public places, nor of the dead; no father was to expect his own son to maintain him if he had not brought him up to some trade or occupation; no one was to remain neutral (i.e. to hold aloof and take no interest) if there were different parties in the state; no woman was to be extravagant in dress.

Solon's laws were written out on wooden tablets and kept in the Prytaneum, and every citizen took an oath to obey them. When all this was completed, he went off on his travels again for ten years, and died in retirement at Athens in 559 B.C.

Peisistratus.

Solon's laws did not please everyone and the people split into three parties—men of the shore, the plain, and the hills. In 561 B.C. an ambitious noble called Peisistratus put himself at the head of the hillmen, who were poor and discontented. One day he drove into the market-place and pointed to wounds inflicted, he said, by his enemies. This was not true, for he had wounded himself in order to deceive the people, but it was believed, and he was given a bodyguard of fifty men, soon increased to four hundred, with whose help he seized the Acropolis (the hill with steep sides in the middle of Athens) and then, with the support of the hillmen, made himself tyrant.

The word 'tyrant' does not mean a cruel, overbearing oppressor, though a tyrant *may* be that; it means a man who rules without being checked or controlled by the state. Many Greek cities at one time or another came under the power of tyrants, who often brought them fame, splendour and prosperity. Peisistratus, who now became tyrant of Athens, really cared about its welfare, and wanted to make

Fig. 13. Women at the well (notice that the *women's* flesh was painted white on black figured vases).

it beautiful, cultured and powerful. He restored the temple to the goddess Athene on the Acropolis; he had Homer's poems re-edited and read at the great festival of the goddess. Clear and pure water was brought to the city from the hills in aqueducts, and work on the land was encouraged. Athenian trade and settlements now reached to the Hellespont,[1] and other cities must have watched with some envy ships passing, heavily laden, to and from Athens, showing how rich and important she was becoming.

Peisistratus had enemies in Athens; he was twice exiled and twice recalled, and died in Athens in 527 B.C. His son

---

[1] Now called the Dardanelles.

Hippias then became tyrant, but when he grew cruel and suspicious he was exiled. This was a good thing, for the Athenians were now free from the dictation of a tyranny.

Cleisthenes.

In about 508 B.C. a noble called Cleisthenes came forward, and, building on the good laws of the past, added something which made Athens a true democracy. Solon, in dividing the people into classes, had given the greatest influence in the state to men of wealth, but Cleisthenes altered this; he divided the people into demes or parishes, grouped in such a way that the old divisions were broken up, and free men of all ranks, rich and poor, were drawn together in their duties towards the state. They voted for the archons and for a Council of five hundred members (fifty for each tribe), whose decisions had to be approved by the Assembly of the People. Each citizen felt that he took a real part in the government; each was expected to give as well as to get; and (since the Council was open to all men over thirty) each knew that he could rise to a high place in the service of his city.

Fig. 14. Dress of an Athenian woman in about 500 B.C.

This brings us to a wonderful time in the life of Athens. Instead of remaining fixed like Sparta, she had changed and grown towards freedom. Her architects, sculptors and craftsmen were at work bringing beauty into the city and the lives of the people, and she shared with other Greek states the wonders which colonization and travel were revealing to the world.

VI

PERSIA AND THE FIRST INVASION OF GREECE

THE RISE OF PERSIA

The Eastern Empires.

In order to understand this chapter, we must go back nearly 100 years to about 600 B.C. and look again at the Eastern Empires the history of which was outlined in the Introductory Chapter of this book (see Map 1).

In Mesopotamia, Assyria with its capital Nineveh had already fallen (612 B.C.) and had become part of the Babylonian Empire under King Nebuchadnezzar (605–562 B.C.). This was now the greatest empire of the Near East.

Nearly 1000 miles north-west of Babylon was the kingdom of Lydia. Its lands were fertile, it contained gold, and was in a fine position for trade, with the result that its king, Croesus, was fabulously wealthy, and was master of the western part of Asia Minor, including the Greek cities of Ionia, which he had conquered.

Between Babylon and Lydia was another power, Media, which now touched the borders of the kingdom of Croesus. These Medes and their neighbours, the Persians, were closely akin in race, and when the Persians under their king, Cyrus the Great (549–529 B.C.), had proved themselves stronger than the Medes and had conquered them, it was more like the fusing of two nations under one name, Persia, than the overthrow of the one by the other.

Cyrus, with his army of Medes and Persians, now set to work to conquer the other great powers and win their possessions. On the west he conquered Croesus, king of Lydia, and thus became master of his kingdom and empire, including the Greek cities of Ionia. On the S.W. he conquered Babylon, whose great empire now became his. At Babylon he found the Jews who had been carried off into exile from Jerusalem by Nebuchadnezzar nearly sixty years before. Cyrus, who was a wise and merciful ruler, made a decree allowing the Jews to return to Judaea, which was now part of his empire.[1]

After the death of Cyrus, his son reigned for a few years and was succeeded by a great king called Darius, whose empire[2] now included Egypt and extended eastward across the borders of India. Against this great and conquering power, what chance had the Greeks when their turn came?

Darius I (521–486 B.C.).

Darius linked his empire together by great roads leading to Susa, his capital. From Sardis, his headquarters in the west, there was a road 1500 miles long, guarded on mountain passes and at river fords by the royal troops. The journey took three months, but urgent messages could be carried to and from Susa in a week, for there were posting-stations and hostelries at intervals of fourteen miles where riders on swift horses were ready, day and night, to carry on the message. As the last of these relay-riders neared his goal, he could see beyond him a fertile, well-watered plain, with mountains in the distance. In this plain stood the great city of Susa, said by a Greek writer to be fifteen or twenty miles round. In it was a huge mound or platform, on which stood the palace of the king. There the messenger would mount the great stairway, pass the royal guards and enter a lofty pillared hall where the king, seated on his throne of

---

[1] His decree is given in the book of Ezra in the Old Testament, chapter i, verses 1–4, and is followed by an account of the return.
[2] See Map 11.

gold and silver, and surrounded by his counsellors and scribes, received from his subjects gold, incense, ebony, ivory and tribute of many kinds. Here the king gave audience to envoys from his dominions, or to his satraps (the Persian governors set over the twenty divisions of his empire)—or

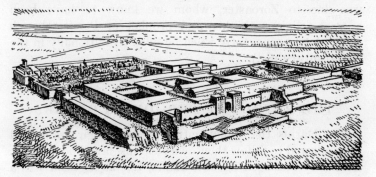

Fig. 15. The palace of Darius I at Susa (reconstruction).

to special officials whom the Greeks called his 'Eyes' and his 'Ears'—men who went about and watched satrap and subject to see if there was anything to report. Everything was in Darius' hands and his word was law, but in spite of this absolute power, he was a wise ruler and, for an Eastern, moderate in his dealings with his people—unless they rebelled.

The Persian religion.

In Persia there were no temples to the gods, for the people worshipped only one great Spirit of Good, the god Ahuramazda or Ormuzd, who 'determined the path of the stars, upheld the earth and the firmament, caused the moon to wax and wane, yoked swiftness to winds and clouds, created light and darkness, sleep and waking, morning, noon and night'.[1]

[1] *Cambridge Ancient History*, vol. iv, p. 207.

On fire-altars on the mountains a sacred flame was lighted, for this was the symbol of the god. Against him worked the Spirit of Evil, Ahriman, fated in the end to be conquered by the Spirit of Good. This was a high religion, more spiritual than the Greek. Much of this teaching was due to Zoroaster, whom we know to have been a great religious thinker and prophet of Persia, though we do not know exactly when he lived (traditionally in the sixth century B.C.).

THE REVOLT OF THE IONIAN GREEKS

Under Darius the Ionian cities pursued their trade and were allowed to follow their own customs, laws and religion. Each city managed its own affairs, but at its head was a Greek tyrant appointed by the king—a form of government loved by Persia but detested by the democratic Greeks. Moreover, the satrap of the district was there to see that they were loyal to the king, paid their due tribute, and served in his army and navy when required.

The Greeks chafed at their loss of freedom, and in 499 B.C. rebellion broke out. It started at Miletus, the leading Ionian city, and then, one after another, the other cities, fired with the hope of freedom, drove out their tyrants. Sparta was asked to aid them and refused, but Athens sent twenty ships and Eretria in Euboea sent five, with which they helped the Ionians to attack Sardis. They had taken all of it except the citadel when a soldier (probably by accident) set fire to one of the houses which were thatched with reeds and straw. The result was that the city was soon in flames. After this the townsfolk seem to have come to some arrangement with the Persians, and the Athenians and Eretrians sailed home.

The famous Greek historian, Herodotus,[1] gives a vivid account of Darius' feelings on hearing the news:

He took no notice of the Ionians—they would not escape punishment, but 'Who', he said, 'are the Athenians?' On being told, he asked for his bow, laid an arrow on it, and shooting it into the sky, he called on Zeus[2] to grant him vengeance on the Athenians. Then he bade one of his servants say to him thrice each time he dined, 'Master, remember the Athenians'.

Darius gathered his forces and after four years succeeded in quelling the rebellious cities. He punished Miletus with the utmost severity; the men were killed, the women and children were sent away to Susa, and a Persian garrison was stationed in the citadel. Athens felt the fall of Miletus bitterly, and knew that her turn would come next.

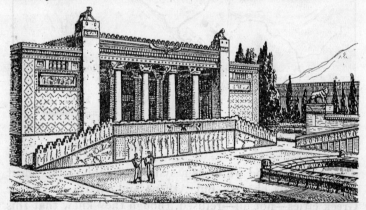

Fig. 16. Part of the Royal Palace at Persepolis (reconstruction).

[1] Herodotus, who was born in about 484 B.C. in one of the cities of Asia Minor, wrote a history of the struggle between Asia and Greece. Modern writers doubt some of his statements, but his account of the Persian wars is so famous for its vividness and picturesque detail, that it has been used freely for this chapter and the next. See Appendix, Note 2.

[2] Herodotus uses the name of the greatest Greek god to express the Persian god, Ormuzd.

THE FIRST PERSIAN INVASION

Darius' first attempt to invade Greece was a failure, for a great storm off Mount Athos destroyed two hundred of his ships, and the rest of the army and navy had to retreat.

Two years later, he was ready to try again. First he sent heralds to the Aegean islands and the cities of Greece to

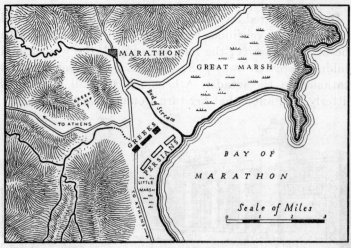

Map 5. Marathon.

demand earth and water as a symbol of submission. Most of the islands obeyed, but Athens and Sparta and other Greek cities—not all—refused, though they knew that this meant war.

Darius now sent his fleet of 600 ships to Eretria in the island of Euboea and the army landed. For six days the citizens fought back the attack; then two traitors among them opened the gates to the enemy, who took and plundered the city, burnt its temples, and carried off the people into slavery, as Darius had commanded.

The Persian fleet moved on to Marathon on the east coast of Attica, about twenty-two miles from Athens, and landed part of their army on the coastal plain. It has been suggested that they did this in order to draw off the troops from Athens, for there was a party in the city which wanted to bring back the tyrant Hippias (p. 44), who had come on one of the Persian ships, hoping to rule again in Athens, by the aid of the Persians. His party was now plotting with the Persians to admit them into the undefended city.

Athens sent to Sparta her swift despatch-runner, Pheidippides,[1] who covered one hundred and forty miles in forty-eight hours and delivered this urgent appeal for help. 'Lacedaemonians,[2] the Athenians beg you not to stand by and see a most ancient city of Greece brought into bondage to barbarians. Already Eretria is enslaved and Greece is weakened by the loss of a notable city.' But Sparta was celebrating a religious festival, whose sacred laws forbade her to set out before the full moon.

Athens was in great danger, for delay and hesitation would bring the Persians to the attack, and the city was unwalled. Under the commander-in-chief, Callimachus, were ten generals, one of whom, Miltiades, had already urged him to oppose the enemy at their landing-place. His lead was now followed, and, after a day's march, 9000 Athenian soldiers stood on the hills near Marathon, looking down on the plain between them and the sea. They were alone and unaided except for one thousand men sent there by the little city of Plataea in Boeotia, which had put herself under the protection of Athens twenty years before.

Below them, between two and three miles away, were the Persian ships. The view is held that the cavalry had been

[1] His story is told by Browning in his poem 'Pheidippides'.
[2] Lacedaemon. This word sometimes stands for Sparta; sometimes (as here) for the whole of Laconia, of which Sparta was the centre.

re-embarked in order to make a sudden attack on Athens. The infantry was drawn up on the plain near the sea in a wide-stretched line. Again Callimachus held a council, and his generals were divided between delay and action, five against five. Again Miltiades urged a bold and swift attack, for Athens was in the greatest danger of her history, and this moment must decide her fate. Callimachus decided to attack. He drew up his line ready to attack the enemy, making it nearly the same length as the Persian line, strong on the wings but only a few lines deep in the long, thin centre.

The signal was given and the Greek line went forward at a run against the enemy. The Persians thought they must be mad; they joined battle and were astonished to find themselves driven back on the wings, though they had easily forced the Greek centre toward the hills. Then the Greek wings, careful not to pursue their enemy too far, wheeled round and routed the victorious Persian centre in an attack in which many of the enemy fell. The remaining Persians fled to their ships, pursued by the Greeks, who in a hand-to-hand fight killed many of them and took seven ships.

Herodotus quotes a rumour that, as they sailed, a shield was seen to flash from a mountain behind Marathon between it and Athens; this was said to be a sign from the traitors in the city, to show the Persians that they could enter.

The Persians rounded the coast, and reached the eastern harbour of Athens, only to find that the Athenians had marched in hot haste from Marathon, and were there before them. Their success seems to have caused the plot to cool down, and the Persians on learning this sailed home.

When these things had been accomplished, two thousand Spartans came after the full moon to Athens, and thence to Marathon to see the battlefield. Here they praised the Athenians for their achievement and then went back to Sparta.

This was not a crushing defeat for Persia, as only a portion of her forces took part in the battle, and she had immense numbers to draw on at home, but the name of Athens was now famous seeing that, almost unaided, she had forced the dreaded Persians to withdraw.

VII

THE SECOND PERSIAN INVASION (480 B.C.)
(See footnote 1, p. 49)

The Preparations.

Ten years later the Persians again invaded Greece. This time their attack was not against Athens and Euboea alone, but against Greece as a whole. Sparta was now the leading state, and was ready to take her full share in the war. Athens, however, brought to the contest a navy and a knowledge of the sea, which won the war for Greece. One of her statesmen, called Themistocles, had seen in good time that the danger would come and that victory would fall to the side that had command of the sea. There was a mine in Attica which was producing quantities of silver, and Themistocles persuaded the Athenians to become sea-minded, and to spend this wealth on building triremes,[1] warships equipped with many oars and a great sail. Athens had now a far greater navy than any other state in Greece.

On the Persian side, Darius was also making ready for war, but he died in 486 B.C. and was succeeded by his son, Xerxes, who was weak and vain, and inherited none of his father's greatness. He carried on preparations for war on a vast scale. He decided that his army, drawn from the forty-six nations of his empire, must not be exposed to the stormy

[1] *Triremes.* See Appendix, Note 3, for further explanation of this word.

Aegean, but must march round the coast while the navy kept in touch with it by sea. A canal was cut for the navy through the storm-swept isthmus of Mt Athos (Map 3), where the ships of Darius had been wrecked twelve years before, and two bridges of boats were made across the Hellespont for the safe crossing of the army.

Fig. 17. One of the body-guard of the Persian king (from a vase painting).

Meanwhile the army had collected at Sardis, and here Xerxes received news that the first bridge had been destroyed by a tempest. Herodotus tells us that in his rage Xerxes ordered that the engineers should be beheaded, and the waters lashed with a scourge three hundred times. These pompous words were then uttered over the strait: 'Thou bitter water! Thy master inflicts this punishment on thee, because thou hast wronged him who never wronged thee. King Xerxes will cross thee whether thou wilt or not; it is right that no man should sacrifice to thee, for thou art an unruly and briny river!' He immediately had new bridges made of triremes and other boats, surmounted by strong ropes and covered with a roadway of planks, heaped with brushwood and earth stamped down, and hedged on both sides by a wooden palisade so that the horses and other animals should not be frightened by the sea.

The March of the Army.

When all was ready, the army set out from Sardis. First came the baggage animals, and the troops of many nations—more than half of the whole army. They were followed by

Persian cavalry and spearmen, followed by ten horses of unusual size with gorgeous trappings; then came eight white horses and the chariot sacred to Ormuzd (p. 47)— empty and guided by a charioteer on foot, for no mortal

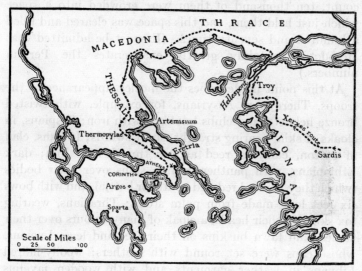

Map 6. Land march of Xerxes.

might mount its seat. After it came Xerxes himself in a chariot, followed by his spearmen and more horsemen, and by 10,000 Persians on foot splendidly equipped. (Herodotus tells us that they were called the Immortals because any losses amongst them were at once made up in order to maintain their full number.)

The army arrived at the Hellespont, and at last the day came for the crossing. As the sun rose, Xerxes, seated on a throne of white marble overlooking the strait, poured an offering into the sea from a golden cup, and prayed with his face to the sun that nothing should stop him from conquering Europe to its farthest limits. Then the long line began to move across the bridge, while the baggage and beasts of burden crossed on a second line of boats. They marched westward and came to a great plain in Thrace where Xerxes numbered his foot-soldiers. As there were far too many to count, ten thousand of them were crowded into a space which just held them, and this space was cleared and filled a hundred and seventy times. (It must be admitted that Herodotus certainly greatly exaggerates the Persian numbers.)

At this point he describes the motley appearance of the troops. There were Assyrians, for example, with twisted bronze helmets, and clubs knobbed with iron; Caspians, in cloaks of skin, bearing straight, short swords; Indians, clad in cotton, carrying reed arrows tipped with iron; dark Ethiopians, with panther or lion skins over their bodies (which they painted red and white for battle), and with bows six feet long made from palm stems; Thracians, wearing fox skins on their heads, a cloak of many colours over their tunics, and fawn buskins on their feet and legs; Lycians, whose caps were set round with feathers; woolly-haired Libyans in leather garments and with wooden javelins charred at the end; and many more.

Meanwhile representatives from many of the Greek cities held a meeting at the Isthmus of Corinth, and decided to form an army and put it under the command of Leonidas, one of the two Spartan kings. Athens felt that she had the right to the command of the united navy but, as many of the states wanted Sparta to have it, Athens gave way because of the peril threatening them all.

The Battle of Thermopylae (480 B.C.).

Xerxes, who had passed through Thrace and Macedonia, now marched southward, conquering as he went, until he came to a place called Thermopylae, a narrow pass between

sea and mountains, which has been called the Gateway of
Greece. To his surprise he found it shut and blocked against
him by Leonidas with about seven thousand Greeks including, among others, three hundred true-born Spartans, a
large number of Peloponnesian troops and some Boeotians.
The Spartans were in the front of the Greek line—so
Xerxes' spies reported—and did not seem in the least
fluttered or dismayed. They were busy at games and
gymnastics, or were combing their long hair, as always
before a battle.

Xerxes was amazed and waited for four days, expecting
the enemy to withdraw. Then he ordered his men to attack,
took his place on a throne and watched. For two days the
Persians (even the Immortals) were driven back, and the
Greeks still held the pass. Xerxes was astounded and three
times in those two days—so it was said—he leaped from the
throne in fear for his troops.

A way over the mountains to the south of the pass was
being guarded by a thousand men of Phocis, a small Greek
state which had offered this service. A native of the district,
called Ephialtes, turning traitor, showed the Persians the
way across, and on the third morning at dawn, the Phocians
heard the tramp of the enemy's troops over the fallen oak
leaves of the forest. They fled, and the Persians marched on.
On hearing this, Leonidas dismissed his allies (possibly
hoping that they could attack the Persians as they came
down in his rear) and he himself remained with his Spartans
together with some Boeotians (perhaps two thousand in
all) to hold the pass. They were warned that when the
Persians shot their arrows, the sun itself was hidden by their
multitude. 'Good news!' called one of them. 'We shall be
fighting in the shade.' And that was the spirit in which they
faced the tremendous struggle that followed. Leonidas was
slain, and his men were gradually driven back, surrounded

and killed. Over their burial-place on the battle-field, a memorial was set up later, with the inscription:

> Bear news to Sparta, stranger passing by,
> That here, obedient to her words, we lie.

Xerxes marched on to Athens and found it almost empty. The non-combatants had sailed for safety to the neighbouring islands of Salamis and Aegina, for this (said Themistocles) was the meaning of the oracle at Delphi which had counselled them to trust to their wooden walls (i.e. to their ships and a victory by sea). Xerxes seized the city from the few defenders who remained in it, and burnt down its temples and houses; at last Athens was punished and Sardis was avenged. He sent the news triumphantly to Susa, and the streets rang with rejoicing, and were strewn with myrtle boughs.

Meanwhile the Greek and Persian navies had been watching and fighting each other off the coast, and were drawing southwards. The Athenians had sent 180 ships, whereas no other state had sent more than thirty, and most of them far fewer than that.

The Battle of Salamis (480 B.C.).

To the west of Athens the island of Salamis blocks in a bay, so that the bay is almost like a lake with a narrow strait at each side. Here were gathered the Greek ships. Themistocles knew that the Peloponnesian commanders wanted to withdraw to Corinth and join their land forces, which had hurriedly built a wall across the isthmus to protect them. This would mean not only the ruin of the Athenian refugees, but of Greece too, for her only hope was to destroy the Persian ships. Therefore Themistocles sent a messenger to Xerxes pretending to be friendly, and urging him to attack quickly, as otherwise the Greek ships in the

bay would slip away before night. Xerxes fell into the trap
and decided to bottle up the enemy's ships. He sat on a
throne placed on a hill-slope overlooking the eastern strait,
surrounded by his scribes, ready to take notes about the
victory. West of the strait were others waiting—the
fugitives from Athens on the island of Salamis, whose fate
hung on the battle.

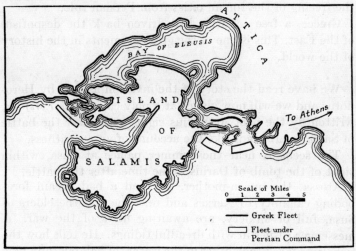

Map 7. Salamis.

At break of day the Persian fleet moved forward, and the
Greeks advanced to meet them. As the Persian lines entered
the narrowing waters, they became crowded and helpless;
they were driven, side to side and end to end, thrown into
confusion by their own numbers and by the onset of the
Greek ships. Before Xerxes' eyes, two hundred of his ships
were sunk or destroyed and his men killed or drowned. At
sunset all was over, and before dawn the remnant of his
navy fled to the Hellespont. Xerxes returned homeward
by the land route with his soldiers, many of whom died

from famine and pestilence. The survivors crossed the Hellespont, and stood once more in Asia.

Xerxes left behind him one of his generals with a large army, which was beaten in a great battle at Plataea in Boeotia—the end of the Persians in Greece. In the same year (479 B.C.) the Greeks won a victory over the Persian fleet on the coast of Asia Minor, which was the beginning of the freeing of the Ionian cities from Persian rule.

Greece, a free country, had driven back the despotism of the East. This is one of the great moments in the history of the world.

We have read the story of the invasion as told by Herodotus and we will now glance at a play called *The Persians*, written by the poet Aeschylus eight years after the battle of Salamis. It reads like the account of an eyewitness.

The scene is near the summer palace at Susa, within sight of the tomb of Darius, some time after the battle.

Atossa, the queen-mother, has had a bad dream foreboding calamity to Xerxes and now she and the elders of Susa, full of anxiety, are awaiting news of the war. A messenger rushes in with dreadful tidings. He tells how the two fleets faced each other in the waters of Salamis, and how the Greeks advanced to the battle with a chant of triumph and the cry:

> Oh, sons of Greece,
> Go forth. Fight for the freedom of your land,
> Your children and your wives, and save the shrines
> Of your ancestral gods. All is at stake!

Then in the battle that followed, the Persian ships had been wrecked or taken, and the men drowned or killed under the gaze of Xerxes.

The queen, clad in robes of mourning, makes offerings to the dead, and bids the elders invoke Darius to return to

earth and counsel them. His ghost appears, and bewails
the folly of Xerxes, which has brought such ruin to his
country, and he tells them that Persia's only hope is never
again to assail the land of Greece. As for their punishment:

> They went to Hellas, and they had the heart
> To wrong the images of gods, to burn the shrines
> And temples, and to dash the altars down.
> Therefore they suffer.

The ghost disappears—shade of a mighty king—and
Xerxes returns with robes rent—a sorry figure, lacking the
greatness of Darius and the dignity of the queen. The play
ends in cries of woe and loss.

We can realize the feelings of the Athenian audience if
we imagine a play on the Spanish Armada (with its scene in
the palace of King Philip) performed before an English
audience soon after the enemy had been repelled from our
shores.

VIII

ATHENS AND HER EMPIRE

ATHENS AFTER THE PERSIAN WARS

The fame of Athens had risen by leaps and bounds during
the war. Other states had been half-hearted or had held
back, thinking of themselves, but Athens had thrown herself into the danger, showing the utmost courage and re-
source, and refusing to yield to misfortune. She had saved
Greece against the first invasion by driving off the Persians
at Marathon, and, in the second, by taking from Persia the
command of the sea, and so winning the war. On the wave
of her pride and fame for this great deed, she rose to high

power, and to a vigorous life, full of happiness, prosperity and beauty, as we shall see in this chapter and the next.

When the Athenian refugees returned home, they found the countryside laid waste and the houses of the city in ruins. They began to rebuild the houses, and to make a new wall round the city, but the Spartans sent envoys at once, asking them not to build this wall, as it would turn the city into a stronghold for the Persians if they came again. Themistocles knew that this was not the real reason, and he immediately put men, women and children on to the work, using any stones or fragments of broken columns that they could lay hands on, and he himself went to Sparta, having first arranged that the other Athenian envoys, who were to join him, should not start until the wall was high enough for defence. The result was that while the Spartans went on enquiring and protesting, and Themistocles went on explaining and saying how surprised he was at the delay, the wall was finished and the Spartans had to accept the fact. Themistocles then fortified the Piraeus, which was situated five miles to the south-west of Athens and now became its chief port (Map 8).

THE CONFEDERACY OF DELOS

The Greek islands and cities on the shores of the Aegean, knowing that unprotected they would never be safe from Persia, asked Athens to become their leader in a league or confederacy of sea states. Athens gladly consented, and in 478 B.C. the league was formed with its headquarters at Delos, a small island in the Aegean, said to be Apollo's birthplace, where all the Ionians gathered to honour him. Here the League council deliberated and its funds were stored; each state was to contribute one or more ships, and those which could not afford this were to contribute money each year. As time went on, Athens began to force states into the League and to subdue those that tried to break away. The treasury was moved from Delos to Athens, for, though Delos was an island sacred to Apollo and should have been safe from attack, the Athenians said that it might be raided by Persian ships, and that the treasure would be safer under their own control. Through this and other important changes, the League of Delos, twenty-four years after its formation, had become the Athenian empire.

PERICLES AND THE REBUILDING
OF ATHENS

Themistocles had shown himself to be a man of a most acute mind, quick at seeing what might happen, clever in meeting danger and difficulty, and unscrupulous in attaining his ends. We have seen him at the height of his power, and we now have to face his fall.

Fig. 18. The Acropolis (restored).

If men became unpopular or were distrusted in Athens, any citizen could, once a year, write one such name on a piece of broken pottery, and if 6000 voted the man named

most often[1] on these fragments (Gr. 'ostraka') was ostra-
cized (i.e. banished) for a number of years. This happened
to Themistocles, who then went to Argos, and, while he was
there, was suspected by the Athenians of having had
treacherous dealings with Persia, a charge which was never
actually proved. He did not go to Athens to stand his trial,
but left Greece, and, after many wanderings, came at last
to the court of Persia, where he was treated with honour
and given a home in Asia Minor. Here he died.

We now turn to another statesman, Pericles, serious and
self-controlled, of noble mind and presence, aristocratic in
his ways and democratic in his sympathies, and a great
orator. He did not court popular favour, but stood aloof
from it in a manner that was dignified and reserved, so that
men called him 'the Olympian'. For thirty years he guided
the affairs of Athens.

He first tried to persuade the states of the Greek mainland
to join in a league of free cities, and to restore all the temples
which had been destroyed in the war, as a thank-offering for the
safety of Greece. When the Peloponnesians refused, Pericles
turned his thoughts to the rebuilding of the temples in
Athens. Towards the cost of this he used part of the tribute
money of the League of Delos, and when certain Athenians
objected, he maintained that if the islands and cities were
safe from Persia, Athens, as head of the League, had done
all that was required. We should probably agree with the
objectors, but Pericles had his way, and proceeded to make
Athens the most beautiful city in Greece. In about twenty
years, the steep and rocky hill of the Acropolis was crowned
by temples and statues, and must have looked very lovely
in the clear Athenian air, and in its setting of mountain and
sea, since the buildings were made of marble and were
painted in parts with bright colours. The western slope led

---

[1] Another view is that there had to be 6000 votes against one individual.

ivory or stone. These men ran their own businesses, often helped by apprentices and slaves.[1]

Most interesting of all was the Potters' quarter. Here on a potter's wheel were made clay vases of all shapes and kinds, such as jars for wine, oil or honey, drinking cups and mixing bowls, scent bottles and ointment boxes. The Greek potter had a genius for making vases of lovely shapes which are copied to-day, and with him worked well-known artists who decorated the vases with scenes of Greek mythology or daily life, done in black on the reddish clay. From the time of the Persian wars the figures were left unpainted, and the background or spaces between them were filled in with black paint. Potter and painter were proud of their work and often signed it—'Erginos made me', 'Aeson drew me'. It is no wonder that the Greeks loved to use these vases in their daily life; they were also exported in large quantities.

Fig. 21. An amphora (jar to hold wine, corn or oil). A figure of Victory pours out wine for a warrior armed for battle.

Many of the buildings in this lower part of Athens were one or two storeys high, with flat roofs, and no windows on the street. These were the homes of the people, and were entered by a passage leading to a courtyard open to the sky, edged with porticoes and rooms. The houses and furniture were of great simplicity, for the Athenians did not spend their money on luxury and display, though nothing was too good for their public buildings and the temples of the gods.

---

[1] There were many slaves in Greece, mostly foreigners captured in war or bought. On the whole they were well treated in Athens, except in the silver mines, where they worked under very bad conditions.

The mistress of the house spent most of her time at home, spinning and weaving, making her own clothes and her husband's, and directing the work of the household slaves. Her education had been meagre in the extreme; she knew nothing of politics, and had few chances of learning anything of the outside world or of meeting people, and she never went out-of-doors unattended. Her daughters stayed at home, beginning a life that was to be as limited as her own, but her sons were sent daily to school when they were six, accompanied by a slave called a paidagogos (our word 'pedagogue'). There until they were fourteen they learnt reading, writing and arithmetic; they recited Homer, played the lyre, and trained their bodies in the palaestra (or wrestling school) with dancing and athletic exercises. If the parents were well off, their education continued till they were seventeen or eighteen. Then, like all Athenian citizens, they trained and served for two years in the army.

Fig. 22. A Greek woman with distaff and wool (from a vase painting).

The husband's life was full of interest. He went out early in the morning (for the Athenians were early risers) and spent most of his day in the open air. Trade he left mostly to the metics, but there were big concerns such as mines or the timber trade in which he might have an interest. Then there were all his public duties; he took his turn to serve as juryman in the law courts, and, even when he was not a member of the Council or a high official, he was expected to attend the open-air Assembly of the people in order to give his vote on public questions. Those who were slack about this and preferred loitering in the market-place, were swept from it towards the Assembly by slaves holding a stretched rope smeared with vermilion, which marked their clothes and showed them to be lazily inclined. Pericles had instituted a small fee for service at the law-courts, for

Fig. 23. Girl dancing (from a vase painting).

he wanted every citizen to be able to take his part as juryman, but the older Athenians shook their heads at paying people to do their duty.

Near the Potters' quarter was the agora or market-place, very full in the forenoon when all the country people had set out their produce on their stalls or in their booths. Here they sold their vegetables, fruit and cheese, their wine, poultry and pigs; here, too, were miscellaneous stalls for pottery, shoes and books. Indeed, it was the sort of scene that you expect in a market. But the setting was of unusual beauty, for, above the market, stood the Acropolis with its temples and statues in view; at the side of the agora were colonnades (painted with scenes from the battle of Marathon and the taking of Troy). In fact the agora was what we now call a civic centre and not merely a market-place. Here the Athenians could discuss with their friends the politics of the moment, the news or rumours of the day, and the latest play or statue. There was always something new to see and hear, which made life almost feverishly exciting for the talkative Athenians. In the evening, the chief meal of the day was taken at home, but the women were not admitted to it if guests were present. The women were allowed, however, to go to see tragedies in the theatre and to attend certain festivals, above all the great Panathenaea, held in the summer every four years in honour of Pallas Athene. Chosen Athenian maidens wove for nine months before this festival a large, oblong piece of stuff dyed saffron colour, for a robe to be presented to the goddess.

The first six days of the festival were given up to contests in music, recitation and sports. On the last night there was a torch race in which youths raced with a blazing torch from the altar of Prometheus[1] into the city, the prize falling to the one who arrived first with his torch still alight. At other festivals this was a relay race, in which the torch was passed from one to another all along the team. The prizes for sports were large jars containing fine oil from the olive tree sacred to Athene; these jars were hand-painted with the figure of the goddess on one side, and on the other was often a picture of the event for which the prize had been won.

On the last day a great procession took place. First came a ship on rollers with the saffron robe stretched to its mast like a sail. Then followed maidens with baskets of offerings,

[1] Honoured in Athens as a being of divine descent who had brought fire to earth for the use of mankind.

white bulls for sacrifice, old men with olive branches, and youths on horseback or standing by the horses and chariots.[1] The procession passed up the steep slope of the Acropolis,

Fig. 24. Slave stealing a poet's dog (from a vase painting).

through the great portals, and past the Parthenon to a temple which contained an old and sacred wooden statue of Pallas Athene, on which they laid the saffron robe.

A regatta, of which the details are unknown, brought the festival to an end.

X

GREEK ATHLETICS AND THE OLYMPIC GAMES

Olympia.

In addition to special festivals in honour of the god or goddess of a single city, there were others called Panhellenic,[2] which were attended by Greeks from all over the Greek world. One of these festivals, held at Delphi, has already been

---

[1] This part of the procession was shown on the frieze of the Parthenon.
[2] Hellas: the Greek world. Panhellenic: concerning the whole of Hellas.

described. We will now look at the most famous of them all, which took place at Olympia in Elis on the west coast of the Peloponnese, in honour of Zeus, the greatest of the Greek gods; it was renowned throughout the world for the games and contests which took place at the festival. (Map 3.)

We must remember that athletics were part of the education of every Greek boy and of the life of every Greek man. As the cities grew, great gymnasia were built—not roofed-in buildings as with us, but large sports grounds surrounded

Fig. 25. "Hockey", from a sculpture in relief.

by colonnades, and placed near a stream and a grove of trees for coolness.

The athlete stripped and was then rubbed down with oil to make his limbs supple, and for some of the exercises, such as wrestling, he was sprinkled with dust or powder to keep his body cool and dry. This oil and dust were afterwards scraped off by a little instrument called a strigil.

The exercises consisted of running, wrestling, jumping and throwing the javelin or discus (a flat round disk of stone or metal); there were ball games, too, one of which looks like our hockey. We have pictures on vases showing the trainers standing by, rod in hand, and also a man playing

Olympia, but in different years from the great games, and it seems to have been attended only by women who lived near—a poor, tame affair compared with that of the men.

The Games.

The first event was the chariot race, causing great excitement as the chariots sped round and round the hippodrome on their nine-mile course. This was followed by the

Fig. 26. Leading in the winner. In front is a herald announcing "the horse of Dusneiketos is the winner." An attendant follows with the wreath of Victory and a tripod as a prize. (This is a Panathenaic victory; p. 72.)

horse race, without saddle or stirrup, and by the test in the stadium for all-round athletes (running, jumping, disk- and javelin-throwing), judged as a whole for the prize. On the third day were the boys' events (a foot race, wrestling and boxing); on the fourth day were the men's foot races varying in length from two hundred yards to three miles; we can still see the stone grooves where the runners toed the line; then followed some wrestling and extremely vigorous boxing which were highly popular among the spectators; and finally a race in armour. The last day ended with rejoicings, and with a public banquet at which the victors were entertained.

On the next day all returned to their own cities. The vanquished, according to the poet Pindar, 'reached home by secret ways, stricken by their misfortune'; but the winners were received with joy, since they had brought honour to their city in the sight of the whole of Hellas. Songs of

Fig. 27. The Discobolus (discus thrower).

victory were written in their honour by Pindar and other poets, and were chanted by choirs of men and boys, as the hero, clad in purple, drove in a chariot to the temple of the chief god of the city, to dedicate to him his wreath of olive. At Athens he had a reward, together with a right to a place of honour at public festivals, and to free meals in the Prytaneum (town hall) if he had need of them. Above all, if he had won three events in the games, his statue could be set up in Olympia itself.

This festival was so important in the eyes of the Greeks that when they wanted to say in what year any event happened, they calculated from 776 B.C., the date of the first Olympic festival; and the games connected with it were—and are—so famous that nowadays international sports which are held in the various countries of the modern world are called the Olympic Games.

Fig. 28. The *modern* stadium at Athens.

XI

THE GREEK DRAMA

THE FESTIVAL OF DIONYSUS

Nowadays when we go to a *theatre*, we listen to the music from the *orchestra* (placed in a narrow line between stalls and stage); we see and hear the actors if it is a *tragedy* or *comedy*, and the *chorus* if it is an opera or a musical play. They perform in front of *scenery* more or less elaborate.

The words in italics are derived from the Greek, but we must clear our minds of their modern meanings, and see what they meant for the Greeks themselves nearly 2400 years ago. The description that follows applies to Greek theatres generally, but our actual visit is to the theatre at Athens in the great days of Greek tragedy.

At the end of March each year there was a great festival to Dionysus, the god of the vine, in whose honour the drama grew up. On each of three days of the festival, at dawn, the people flocked into a great open space, almost circular and with descending tiers of seats, dug out of the side of the Acropolis. This was the theatre of Dionysus. The seats were backless, undivided, narrow, and hard. It was advisable to bring a cushion, and provisions for the whole day, but not to bring any protection from the sun, though the theatre faced south, as parasols were not popular with the row behind. Gradually the auditorium, containing about fifteen thousand seats, filled up—a scene gay with the garments of bright colours worn on festal occasions, as well as the customary white. As the time for the performance approached, the front seats, which were reserved for the people whom the city wished to honour, began to fill with officials, priests, generals, boys whose fathers had fallen in battle for the city, ambassadors from foreign states, and, in the chief seat of honour, the priest of Dionysus.

Below the front row of seats there was a large, level, circular space, which was called the orchestra (dancing floor) with the altar of Dionysus in the centre. Beyond this was probably a low platform with a background[1]

---

[1] In the earliest days the background was only a tent or hut (Greek: 'skene') for the actor to change in. Later this developed into quite elaborate buildings which served as the *scene* or scenery for the acting. We do not know the exact appearance of the stage buildings at the time of the three great writers of tragedy, and some scholars think that there was no platform in these early days.

which usually represented the front of a palace, as the plays often dealt with royal families, but the poet was not limited to such a background if he wanted the front of a temple or natural scenery. There was no curtain.

By this time the judges who were to award the prizes were in their seats, for the festival was a contest for the best written and best produced plays. Three poets had been

Fig. 29. A Greek theatre (reconstruction). This drawing is conjectural. See footnote, p. 80.

selected, one for each day's performance—and a long day too, since each poet had written three tragedies (sometimes connected with the same family or course of events but each able to stand alone as a separate play), to be followed by a burlesque called a satyric drama, which afforded amusing relief after the tragedies. The chorus of these plays represented satyrs, frolicsome creatures, with snub noses, pointed ears, hoofs and tails; they were connected with the worship of Dionysus.

GREEK TRAGEDY

The Plays and their Writers.

The three great writers of Greek tragedy were

525–456 B.C. Aeschylus (who fought with the infantry at Marathon).

496–406 B.C. Sophocles (who was a commander in one of the later wars of Athens).

c. 480–406 B.C. Euripides.

These poets were very different. Aeschylus was rugged and grand; Sophocles was more polished and calm; Euripides' plots moved quickly and were full of human interest. Between them they wrote some of the greatest literature of the world. The plots of their plays were usually taken from mythology or early history—from stories of gods and heroes, or from the Trojan war and its consequences; this helped many of the audience to follow the plot.

The Play.

We will imagine ourselves present at a performance of *The Antigone* of Sophocles, a very famous play with a plot taken from the story of Thebes.

The chief characters (all are of the royal House of Thebes) are *Antigone* and *Ismene*, sisters of Eteocles and Polynices, who are now dead; *Creon*, their uncle, now king of Thebes; *Haemon*, his son, betrothed to Antigone. There is a *Chorus* of fifteen Theban elders, and the *scene* is the front of the palace at Thebes. Not more than three characters on the stage have speaking parts in any one scene in a Greek play, but there are often many silent actors (soldiers, courtiers, etc.).

Antigone and Ismene enter. They are represented by men chosen partly for the power and beauty of their voices.

They wear masks to show what sort of character they impersonate, and thick soled shoes to give them height.[1]

The sisters are in mourning garb, for their brothers are dead. Before the opening of the play Eteocles had broken his promise to rule Thebes in turn with Polynices, who then came with an army from Argos against his own city, Thebes. This army had been defeated, and the brothers had fallen by each other's hands in single combat. Creon, their uncle, was now king, and had issued an edict forbidding anyone to bury Polynices on pain of death, since he had come in order to

> Burn with fire his native land, the shrines
> Of his ancestral gods, and shed the blood
> Of kinsmen.

The Greeks believed that the soul of a dead man had no rest until his body was buried, and in this opening scene Antigone tells Ismene that she is determined to bury Polynices or at least to scatter dust over his body, for that will serve for burial. Ismene tries in vain to dissuade her.

They leave the stage, and the chorus of fifteen elders of Thebes enters the orchestra. Here they chant and sing of the battle at the walls of the city, and, as they sing, they stand or move in a solemn dance, showing by their movements, gestures and attitudes, their horror at the deed of Polynices and their joy at the safety of Thebes. (They sing similar odes of joy, fear and warning in the course of the play.)

Creon comes from the palace, easily recognized by his gorgeous regal robes and his train of attendants, and soon after, a watchman enters to tell him that someone has thrown dust on Polynices' body. After a song from the chorus, the watchman comes in again with Antigone whom he has caught

---

[1] This shoe (cothurnus; Engl. buskin) is now thought not to have been used during the great century of Greek drama (the fifth B.C.).

pouring libations on her brother's body in spite of the king's command. Creon and Antigone are now left face to face. He upholds his edict, since it is his duty to the state to check such lawlessness. She glories in her act of piety, for she has done her duty to her kinsman, knowing well that it means her death.

> I did not think the edicts of a *man*
> Had strength to override the laws of *heaven*,
> Unwritten and unfailing, for they live—
> Not now nor yesterday, but for all time,
> Eternal.

Neither yields; it is not merely a conflict between two determined people, but it is a clash between two great duties—to the laws of man and the laws of the gods. Antigone and Ismene, who (against her sister's wish) is ready to share her fate, are led into the palace under a guard. Ismene is released, but Antigone is taken to die in a walled-up chamber. Neither the chorus, with words of counsel, nor Haemon, first with entreaty and then with bitter reproach, can bend the king's will. Finally Creon yields to an old, blind prophet, who warns him that he and his city will suffer terrible punishment from the gods, who are displeased at the rites of burial being refused. Creon buries Polynices, and goes to release Antigone, but it is too late. He finds out that she has died by her own hands and that Haemon has killed himself over her body. Creon is left desolate, fallen from all his happiness and well-being. The last words of the chorus bring home a lesson of the play.

> The greatest part of happiness
> Is to be wise and reverent to the gods.
> Great words of pride are punished with great blows,
> And, in old age, these school men to be wise.

GREEK COMEDY

The greatest writer of comedy was Aristophanes (about 445–388 B.C.). Usually his plays held up to ridicule some well-known man of the day, or the faults of the democracy; or they dealt with some question of politics, peace or war.

In one of these comedies, *The Birds* (with a chorus dressed as birds), the subject of the plot is the building of an imaginary town in the upper air, 'Cloud-cuckoo-town', as a way of escape from the worries of earth. In another play, *The Frogs* (so called from the song of the frogs in the earlier part of the play), Aeschylus and Euripides are compared. A balance is set on the stage into which are spoken weighty lines from Aeschylus and clever ones from Euripides. Aeschylus offers to put two of his own lines in one scale against Euripides, with all his works and his whole family in the other. The judge decides in favour of Aeschylus, since his grave and serious words and thought fit him best to give the state counsel in the troubles which now beset it.

There is no space here to describe these and the other comedies, with their mixture of beauty and coarseness, clever criticism and rough play. They may have been performed in the afternoon at the end of each day or (more probably) they may have had a day to themselves at the end of the great festival.

During the next century comedy changed; coarseness gave place to gentleness, and political abuse to stories of everyday life. The greatest writer of this 'New Comedy', as it was called, was Menander, whose plays were a model for the comic writers of Rome, who in their turn influenced modern comedy (p. 67, part II, The Romans).

XII

THE PELOPONNESIAN WAR. I (431–421 B.C.)

THE RIVAL LEAGUES

We have seen how the Confederacy of Delos developed into the Athenian Empire. This naturally roused ill-feeling in Sparta, for she had long been the leading state in Greece, and now she saw her position threatened, the trade of Corinth and her other Peloponnesian allies in danger, and the Greek cities, once free, 'enslaved', as she called it, in the grip of Athens. She gradually gathered round her a league of mainland states which shared her ideas and her jealousy of Athens and would not leave her friendless, if anything happened.

In 433 B.C. something did happen. Corcyra, an island off the coast of Epirus, had quarrelled with her mother-city, Corinth, and had turned to Athens for help. This affair at Corcyra was the spark that set fire to a mass of material which had been piling up for years, ready to burst into flame. When Athens sent help to Corcyra, Corinth appealed to Sparta, and, after long discussions, war broke out.

On the side of Sparta were almost the whole of the Peloponnese, Corinth and Megara on the isthmus, and all Boeotia except Plataea. She had a large army, trained and drilled to the uttermost, which could be almost sure of victory in a pitched battle. On the side of Athens were a few allies as well as the enforced service of her Empire, much money laid aside for war, many men available for her army, and, above all, her navy and her skilled seamen. As Pericles said, seamanship was an art that could not be practised at odd moments like a hobby; the Athenians had worked hard at it for fifty years and it would take Sparta a long time to catch them up.

The account which follows is taken from Thucydides, one of the greatest of the world's historians, who lived through the whole course of the war, first as a general, then as a careful and vivid recorder of the events which took place up to 411 B.C.

THE FIRST TEN YEARS OF THE WAR (431–421 B.C.)

The Invasion of Attica.

At the end of May, when the corn was ripe, the Spartan forces marched into Attica. On the advice of Pericles, the country people came into Athens for protection, bringing with them their children and wives and their personal

Fig. 30. A peasant on his way to market.

possessions, having sent their sheep and beasts of burden to the islands near. Most of the people had always lived in the country and were heavy at heart and aggrieved at leaving their farms, and the shrines that had always been theirs, for unknown homes in the city. Only a few of them

found refuge in houses; the rest went to live in the empty
spaces of the city, or in the temples and shrines (though
not on the Acropolis), and in the towers in the city walls.
Later they were assigned huts in the space between the
Long Walls and in the Piraeus.

The Spartan army came within seven miles of Athens,
destroying the corn and the farms. Most of the people in
the city, especially the young men, thought that they ought
to go out and stop this at once; they gathered in knots,
disputing hotly, and there was indignation in the city
against Pericles for not leading them out. He wisely refused
to let them fight a land battle, but he sent one hundred
ships plundering and taking towns round the Peloponnese.
The Spartan troops, when their food was exhausted, went
home, but their raids as well as the counter-attacks round
the coast by the Athenians, occurred nearly every year
during this part of the war.

At the end of the year, there was a public funeral in
Athens for those who had fallen. Their bones were carried
in a procession of ten wagons and there was one empty
bier covered with a pall in honour of the unknown warriors
who were missing. This procession was followed by the
famous Funeral Speech of Pericles, in which he spoke in
glowing praise of the city, 'the school of Hellas', for the
whole Greek world learned of her—the city of free men,
lovers of beauty and wisdom. For such a city had these
men of courage, when called to action, died, leaving an
undying memory.

The Plague and the Fall of Pericles.

The next summer Athens was attacked by a plague which
spread quickly in the crowded and unhealthy conditions in
the city. It is fully described by Thucydides, who himself
caught it and recovered. He knew how suddenly it came,

how violent was the fever, how helpless the physicians were against it. Men who recovered (says Thucydides) cherished the idle fancy that no other disease could carry them off. One-quarter of the people died of it, and the population never again reached its former numbers.

In their despair and misery, the people for a time turned against Pericles, unjustly laying the blame on him. His two sons had died of the plague, and he himself, though he had it and survived, never completely recovered his health. Although the people once more turned to him and elected him general, he died in the following year (429 B.C.). Such was the end of Pericles, the leader of Athens in her greatest days, the man who had built up the city and its life after the Persian wars, and had founded the Empire.

During the next eight years the Athenians were on the whole successful, able to beat the enemy's navy, and to keep open the sea-routes for their food supplies, but they missed the wise control of Pericles. The state was like a chariot drawn by horses pulling in different directions, and there was no one like Pericles to guide it now, holding his team in order, keeping watch on the dangers around, and not losing sight of his goal.

Cleon.

Cleon is an example of a new kind of political leader in Athens; he was a demagogue, that is, the kind of leader who by ranting and violence in thought and word could sway the feelings of the people. He was ruthless, self-confident, and clever. Let us take three events which brought out these qualities of his, and see what sort of person now had influence in Athens.

Mitylene.

Mitylene was the leading city on the island of Lesbos, which had revolted from Athens. Cleon persuaded the

Athenian Assembly to send an order at once to kill all the men and enslave all the women and children in the city. On the next day the Athenians repented of this decree, and sent another boat, speeding across the Aegean by night and day, to reverse it. It was only just in time, and the mass of the people were spared. Cleon was left at home, raging at such weakness in dealing with rebels, who—he said—should have been dealt with as they deserved, showing to all that revolt meant death.

The offer of peace.

Under their able and vigorous commander, Demosthenes (not the famous orator, of whom we shall hear later), the Athenians seized a headland called Pylos (425 B.C.) on the west coast of the Peloponnese, and cut off 420 Lacedae-monians in the island of Sphacteria, south of Pylos. The Spartans were so depressed at this seizure of their land and at the blockade of their men that they sent envoys to Athens with offers of peace and friendship. This did not suit the ideas of Cleon and the war party since, now that they had grasped something, they were greedy for more, and they demanded so much that the envoys left Athens with nothing done. How different would have been the history of the city if she had had a wiser counsellor!

Sphacteria.

We next see Cleon again in the Assembly, taunting the generals for letting the affair at Sphacteria drag on. Thu-cydides gives us a lively account of the scene—Cleon, pointing at Nicias, one of the generals, and boasting that he himself could take the island if he were in command; his embarrassment when the Assembly took him at his word; their burst of laughter when at last he declared that he would finish off the affair in twenty days—to be followed by their astonishment when he returned with the Spartan prisoners, the hero of the hour. We are not told whether Demosthenes, who did most of the work, had any share in the praise.

Three years later, Cleon and the brave, successful Spartan commander, Brasidas, were killed in the same engagement. Sparta and Athens were tired after nearly ten years of war, and a peace (called the Peace of Nicias) was arranged by which both sides were to give up their prisoners and conquests (421 B.C.).

This was a restless peace, which was followed almost immediately by disturbances, quarrels, and the making and breaking of alliances—the very opposite of peace.

XIII

THE PELOPONNESIAN WAR. II (416–404 B.C.)

THE EXPEDITION TO SICILY

Syracuse.

We have seen (Chapter III) how Greek cities were built round the coasts of the Mediterranean, especially in Sicily and in the south of Italy. Syracuse, a colony founded from Corinth about 734 B.C., was now by far the strongest city in Sicily. Her tyrants lived in power and magnificence like kings, and attracted many famous men to their courts. Aeschylus had come from Athens, and Pindar from Thebes, and there were so many others and the city was so powerful, and such a centre of art and learning, that she has been called 'The Athens of the West'. In her pride, Syracuse had made war on certain cities of Sicily, and her harsh treatment and overbearing ways were bitterly resented by

them after their long years of freedom. Athens was on
friendly terms with some of the cities, and was anxious
about this growing power of Syracuse. Did it threaten her
corn supply from Sicily, and had the time come for her to
check Syracuse and to turn her own empire towards the
west? We must now return to Athens and see what sort of
men took upon themselves to answer this question.

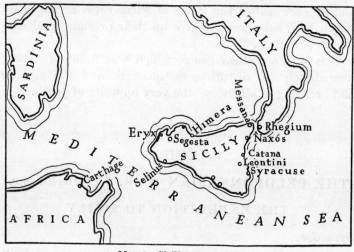

Map 9. Sicilian campaign.

Nicias, in whose name the shortlived peace had been
made, was a religious man, rich, honest and respected, a
lover of peace and moderation. He had shown himself to
be a good general, but he lacked the force and decision needed
in the great task that now fell to him. In this task he had to
work with a man who was his very opposite in character and
ideas.

Alcibiades.

Alcibiades was young, brilliant, and handsome. He had
been born into a life of ease and luxury, and he soon fell

under the spell of flatterers, who told him that he would surpass all other commanders and statesmen, even Pericles himself. The teaching of the philosopher, Socrates, for whom he had real respect and affection, could not outweigh all this flattery nor turn the bent of Alcibiades' own mind. He was unscrupulous and lawless, and did not know what it meant to be straight and honourable, but many of the citizens were dazzled by his eloquence and display, and were ready to follow him in all his ambitious schemes. He was now working against peace, and was forming in his mind the idea of a great campaign in the west. Sicily, Carthage, the coast of Africa, Italy—all these might be won for the Athenian Empire, under his own brilliant and dashing leadership.

In 416 B.C. a quarrel arose between two cities in Sicily—Selinus, which was supported by Syracuse, and Segesta, which was allied with Athens. Messengers came from Segesta, who begged Athens to send help, undertaking to pay the cost of the expedition; in answer to this, envoys were sent from Athens to see if Segesta could carry out her promise. The crews were entertained at one house after another at tables equipped with drinking vessels of gold and silver; quantities of sacred vessels were to be seen, too, in a temple treasury. The Athenians, deeply impressed by all this wealth and influenced by Alcibiades, voted for the expedition. They refused to listen to Nicias when he warned them not to undertake a new war which did not concern them, while their own state was 'still amid the waves'. In charge of the expedition they put Nicias, Alcibiades, and a good practical soldier and general called Lamachus. While the preparations were going on, Athens was startled one morning to find that the Hermae (busts of Hermes on square pillars) which stood in shrines and at the doors of houses, had been secretly defaced and mutilated during the night by unknown hands. Alcibiades and his companions were suspected, for it was the kind of mad behaviour that they indulged in, and the excitement was intense; such sacrilege was a bad omen for the expedition, and might even be part of a plot against the democracy. Still, at midsummer the ships set out, and Alcibiades with them.

The Setting Out.

Thucydides gives a famous description of the expedition. At dawn on the appointed day, the Athenians went to the Piraeus and began to man the ships. Nearly every one in the city went too, to see off friends, kinsmen and sons, with hopes and lamentations—hopes of new gains, lamentations at the fear of not seeing their men again—but they plucked up courage when they looked at the strength and beauty of the fleet. Each trierarch (a citizen who had given and equipped a trireme) had been eager to make his own ship surpass all others in swiftness and beauty, and the fighters—picked men—vied with each other in arms and accoutrements. When the ships were manned and everything was aboard, a trumpet sounded for silence, and all together, led by a herald, offered the customary prayers before sailing, while the throngs on the shore joined in the prayers. Then the crews raised the paean[1] and put to sea (134 triremes and many other vessels, containing 27,000 fighting men). Sailing at first in single file, they raced as far as Aegina, whence they hastened on to Corcyra where the ships of their allies were assembled; from there they started for the west. When they approached Sicily, they heard that very little of the promised money was at Segesta, that the 'golden' sacred vessels had been gilded silver, and that the gold and silver drinking vessels displayed on the tables of their hosts had

---

[1] Paean; a song or chant addressed to Apollo, but also used for any song of praise or triumph.

been collected in Segesta and other cities and carried quickly from house to house, to give a false idea of the riches of the citizens; this was bad news, but they decided to go on with the expedition. Taking the advice of Alcibiades, they did not attack Syracuse at once, but tried first to win over

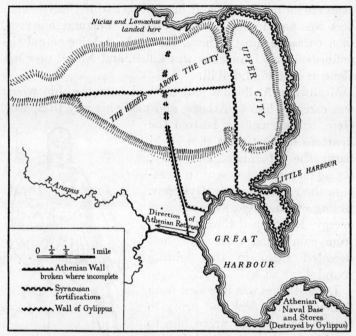

Map 10. Syracuse.

the other cities to their side. This plan, however, was a failure, for only one city, Naxos, received them, and Syracuse had time to prepare her defence. To Naxos came a swift sailing ship from Athens, which took Alcibiades back in order to stand his trial in connection with the mutilation of the Hermae, but the Athenian fleet sailed on to Syracuse, in spite of all these checks, and disappointments, under the command of Nicias, who landed his army and began to hem in the city with a wall from south to north.

The Syracusans were almost in despair, for when they tried to cut off the wall by counter-walls, the Athenians were too quick for them and carried the work on nearer and nearer to the north coast and, in addition to this, the Athenian fleet was now in their Great Harbour. Fortune, however, soon turned against Athens, for in the fighting round the unfinished wall Lamachus was killed, and Nicias, now left alone in command, fell ill.

Meanwhile Alcibiades had escaped from the ship which was carrying him to Athens, and made his way to Sparta. Here, turning traitor, he told the Spartans in what ways they could harm the Athenians and they, acting on his advice, sent to Syracuse their best general, Gylippus. Acting with great vigour and energy, he stopped the Athenians from completing their wall, and defeated them in the fighting round it.

Fig. 31. A Greek soldier.

Demosthenes was now sent from Athens with a fleet and army to help Nicias, and he urged him to get his men down to the Athenian ships in the Great Harbour. Unfortunately, there was an eclipse of the moon just when they were ready to start, and this seemed to the superstitious Nicias a sign that they must stay where they were for twenty-seven days. By the time that he consented to move, the Syracusans had blocked the mouth of the harbour, and the only hope now left to the Athenians was to break through this barrier to the open sea.

The Battle in the Harbour (September, 413 B.C.).

The ships were reached and manned, and a great battle was fought in the harbour. On the narrow waters, crowded by two hundred ships, there could be no order in the fighting; ship engaged ship all over the harbour, and when they closed, the men fought hand to hand, amidst the din of crashing vessels and the loud shouts of command. On the shore, the townsfolk in their city and the Athenians in their camp stood watching the fight, torn between hope and fear. At last the Syracusans drove the Athenian ships to shore, and the crews rushed for safety to their camp.

The Retreat.

The army now began to retreat westward by land, only to find their way blocked by the enemy. Then they turned southwards and on the night of the sixth day of the retreat, the two divisions lost touch in the darkness, and this was the beginning of the end. Demosthenes was caught with his men in an olive grove, and forced to surrender. Nicias, who was ahead with his section, struggled on till he came to a stream and found the enemy facing him on the opposite bank. The men rushed to the water to drink, and many of them, being off their guard, were slain. Nicias and Demosthenes were put to death; many of the prisoners were sent to work in the stone quarries of Syracuse, and those who survived were sold as slaves. A few were freed by their masters for reciting to them speeches or choruses from Euripides and a very few reached home to tell the tale. In spite of the dreadful news, Athens refused to despair and built a new fleet.

By this time Alcibiades had first quarrelled with Sparta, and had then helped Persia who was encouraging the allies of

Athens to revolt. Now, changing sides once more, he offered to come back to Athens, and was actually recalled, but though he helped her to win some successes at sea, he soon fell under suspicion again, and was dismissed and exiled. He withdrew to his castle near the Hellespont, and, later, to Phrygia, where, under orders from Sparta, his house was surrounded by Persians and he was killed.

THE FALL OF ATHENS
(from Xenophon)

Though she had lost most of her allies, Athens fought on for nine more years. She had some important successes at sea, but at last Sparta and Persia brought a great fleet against her at Aegospotami on the Hellespont (405 B.C.) and utterly defeated her. This was the end of fleet and army, money and hope. Lysander, the Spartan commander, forced the last of the allies to submit to him; he blockaded Athens, and cut off her corn supply until she surrendered. He did not destroy the city, since she had done such great service to Greece in her peril in the past, but he obliged her to give up her empire and all her ships except twelve, and to pull down her Long Walls and the fortifications of the Piraeus. Athens must be an ally of Sparta, but otherwise she was free.

For the next eighteen months, there was no peace or safety in this freedom. One party in Athens aimed at bringing the state under an oligarchy (the rule of a few men), and thirty of these oligarchs, led by Critias, gained power; they soon won the name of 'the thirty tyrants'. Under their cruel rule, hundreds of the democrats were killed, and many went into exile, and this confusion and bloodshed did not cease until Critias had been killed in a fight with the democrats, and the king of Sparta had come to Athens to reconcile the two parties. With his help the tyrants were exiled and the democracy was restored (403 B.C.).

XIV

PHILOSOPHY AND MEDICINE

EARLY GREEK PHILOSOPHY

The Ionians.

We will leave for a time the tale of wars and empires and turn to the story of a Greek thinker called Socrates who died soon after the end of the Peloponnesian war. In order to understand his life and teaching, we must go back some 200 years and see what progress had been made by men who had been giving up their lives, not to action but to thought.

The map on p. 15 shows the strip of country called Ionia. It was inhabited by Greeks, who could easily get into touch with the learning of the great empires of the east; in fact it was a good starting-place for travel and adventure in every direction, and these travels brought new knowledge and ideas to the enquiring minds of these Ionians, so that, quite early in their history, they became more advanced than the Greeks of the mainland.

Thales.

The first and greatest of these thinkers of Ionia was a Greek called Thales, who was born about 624 B.C., more than 2500 years ago. We are told that his business as an engineer took him to Egypt, where he spent many years. He returned with such an admiration for Egyptian science that he gave up trade, and turned to the pursuit of knowledge. He studied astronomy, and was able to foretell eclipses; he made a great advance in geometry, for though the Egyptians had already studied it, their geometrical figures were formed by lines and angles of a special size or shape, whereas Thales

7-2

discovered truths which held for *any* figure of the kind that
he was describing; for example, that the angles of *any* triangle were together equal to two right angles; that the angles
at the base of *any* isosceles triangle were equal; and that the
opposite angles formed by the crossing of any two straight
lines were equal. He could also apply geometry to practical
problems, such as calculating the height of a pyramid by
its shadow, or the distance from land of ships at sea.

Thales knew something about magnetism, and the
electricity caused by friction (rubbing one substance against
another). Amber ('electron' in Greek), the hardened sap of
a sort of pine tree found on the shores of the Baltic Sea, was
known for its beauty and was used by the Greek ladies for
necklaces and ornaments. Thales noticed that when the
amber rubbed against the material of the dresses, it attracted
little pieces of hair, straw and dust. He thought that this was
due to a mysterious soul or spirit. Only one other substance
showed a similar power of attracting things; this was
the magnetic lodestone found at Magnesia, in Asia Minor.
There is a story of a shepherd boy of Troy, sheltering under
a rock from the heat of the sun. His iron crook was snatched
from his hand, and it clung to the rock above his head. This,
again, was explained by giving to the iron ore a mysterious
soul or spirit.

These observations of Thales (which were remembered
but not developed in ancient times and the Middle Ages)
were used in A.D. 1600 by an Englishman, Dr Gilbert of
Colchester, who was the first to conduct systematic experi-
ments in the sciences of magnetism and electricity.

In its early period, the name 'philosophy' (love of
wisdom) included science and mathematics. Some of the
philosophers tried to think out the cause and nature of the
world whose wonders they saw around them. Thales, seeing
that life was helped and sustained by water, thought that

water was the first cause of all things. Another thought that the first cause was fire; another, air; another, mist or vapour, of which fire, water, winds, clouds and earth were thicker or thinner forms. Some of the philosophers discovered truths which later became part of scientific thought. For example, one of them held that the world consisted of atoms (particles which could not be broken up into smaller particles) —but in the use of these atoms he was not very scientific, for he thought that the world and its contents were formed by these atoms clashing together as they fell through space. The earth too, had been compared, even by Thales, with a flat disk floating on water, but now some philosophers thought that it might be a sphere, and that it might *not* be the centre round which the heavenly bodies turned. And the sun was much larger than it looked—larger, perhaps, than the whole of the Peloponnese.

While men had been searching for truths in this way, Athens had been growing from a small city to a very important one. When the Persian wars were over, and the city, under the guidance of Pericles, had become famous for its power, its art, and its literature, learned men gathered there from many parts of the Greek world; among these, there was a class of men called Sophists, who undertook to teach, for pay, any subject, and especially grammar (the science of language), literature and rhetoric—studies which would make a man more cultured, and help him to think clearly and speak well in public. Such teaching was apt to be superficial, and to aim at training young men merely to get on in the world and to make a good show of their knowledge.

By this time many philosophers were becoming tired of speculations about the nature of the world, and were now more interested in human philosophy, with its study of the mind and conduct of man. Among famous thinkers of this kind was an Athenian called Socrates, and this is his story.

SOCRATES[1]

Socrates was born near Athens in 469 B.C., and had lived through the great events of the last chapters. He had seen Athens in her triumph and in her downfall, and he loved the city so much that he never left it except when he was called on, as an Athenian citizen, to fight in the Peloponnesian war.

He showed courage and presence of mind in battle, and, on one occasion, he saved the life of Alcibiades by standing over him when he had fallen wounded, and protecting him from his enemies. He could endure hunger and extreme cold, and, in the depth of winter, when other men kept warm their feet and legs with skins and fleeces, he walked barefoot on the ice. One day, in camp, a strange thing happened; from early morning till nightfall he was seen standing alone in deep thought, as though questioning and enquiring within himself. All through the night he stood there until, when the sun rose, he saluted it with a prayer, and departed.

At home, in Athens, too, Socrates was noticeably different from other men. He still cared nothing for his own comfort; he was clumsily made and shabbily dressed, and his face was plain, with a snub nose and prominent eyes, and yet there was always a throng of men round him in the agora, and in other places where men gathered.

By his time the Greeks had become interested in man—his mind, conduct and ideals—and Socrates gave up his life to that part of philosophy which is the search for the truth and wisdom that should guide men's conduct; he was so eager to help others in the same search, so original and

[1] Socrates wrote nothing himself, but his discourses and the account of his last days were written down by his pupil, the philosopher, Plato.

unexpected and clear-sighted that his words caught the attention of his hearers, and clung to their minds far more than eloquence. He took no money for his teaching, since he claimed to be only a fellow-seeker of knowledge with his followers, and he was utterly astonished when his impetuous friend, Chaerephon, went to Delphi to ask whether any man was wiser than Socrates, and was told that no man was wiser. 'I went first to a politician,' said Socrates, 'but found that he was not wiser though everyone, including himself, thought so, and then I went to one man after another, making enemies every day, and finally to poets and craftsmen, who were skilled in their art, but not truly wise. So at last I decided that the oracle meant that those people are wisest who, like me, know that their wisdom amounts to nothing.'

Socrates thought that men did evil because they were ignorant of the good, and so he tried to guide them to the truth by such questions as 'What are piety, justice, the noble and the base, the beautiful and the ugly?' He led them on by question and answer to realize in what way their ideas had been shallow or confused, and to think for themselves in order to get to the root of the matter. He never lectured to them or dictated his own ideas—he was a searcher like themselves. The Sophists were annoyed with him when he pretended to want to learn from them and then entangled them with his questions, but the young men who followed him loved his wit and charm and were devoted to him.

After thirty years of such teaching, some of the Athenians began to think that it was harmful to the state. His followers, they said, had sometimes turned out badly, especially Alcibiades, the traitor, and Critias, the tyrant. There were fathers who grumbled because they thought their sons were wasting their time and becoming unsettled, and many other people's minds were ruffled by the ways and words of this strange philosopher. They doubted his ideas about the gods, for though he paid them their due rites and prayers, he openly disbelieved the old stories of their wars and bitter hatreds. He often spoke of God, not gods, and of an inner voice—a divine warning—which came to him from time to time when he was contemplating some course of action.

In 399 B.C. he was charged with not believing in the gods of the city, and of introducing new gods, and of corrupting the young men. The penalty for this was death. Though he could easily have escaped from Athens he chose to remain and stand his trial before the jury of five hundred and one Athenian citizens.

He spoke of the oracle, of his inner voice, of his refusal of payment for teaching, and of his service to Athens in urging men not to think so much about money-making and other men's opinion, but to care for the things that mattered —wisdom, truth and the perfection of the soul. He said that he had not run away from his post in war time, and it would be strange conduct if he now ran away, through fear of death, from doing what God had commanded him to do. 'I shall not change my way of life,' he said, 'even if I have to die for it many times.' His speech ended with the words: 'I do believe in the gods as no one of my accusers believes in them; and to you and to God I entrust my cause, to decide it as is best for you and for me.'

He was found guilty by a majority of sixty votes, and then, in accordance with Athenian law, was allowed to propose some other form of punishment. He said that he deserved honour, rather than punishment and he refused the idea of exile, merely offering a fine. He was then condemned to death.

Socrates' friends were allowed to visit him in prison. On the last day, they came at dawn, feeling as though they were about to lose a father, but he refused to let them help him to

escape or to be sad at his death. To him it was the journey
of his soul to a new, unseen world, into the presence of the
gods and perhaps of the great men of the past, and to the
knowledge of the Truth.

When the time came for him to drink the hemlock (for
this poison was to be the method of his death) he prayed
for a prosperous journey, drank the hemlock, and died
without fear calmly. 'This was the end', said one of the
disciples, 'of our friend, of all those whom we have ever
known, the best, the wisest, and most just.'

GREEK MEDICINE

Hippocrates.

We will now turn from the story of Socrates, and his care
for the welfare of men's minds and thought, to the story of
another Greek, about nine years younger than Socrates,
who devoted his life to the care of men's bodies. His name
was Hippocrates, and he has been called the Father of
Medicine. He was born in about 460 B.C., in an island of the
Aegean called Cos, which was a centre of medical learning.
Perhaps his own father and grandfather had been among
the physicians who lived there. We know very little about
the life of Hippocrates, except that he lived to a great age,
and was world famous and had travelled to many places,
including Athens, studying and practising his art. He would
have nothing to do with the charms and other magical
devices which had often been used by so-called physicians
of the past, and he hated guess-work. He watched and
noted down carefully his patient's symptoms and the course
of his illness, and so, from a number of such cases, he built
up a knowledge of the disease itself and its treatment. This
method of reasoning from single examples to a general rule
is called *inductive*, and is a very important scientific method.

Hippocrates made notes on his discoveries, for he wanted to hand down to those who followed him the knowledge which he had gained with so much care. He thought that disease was due to natural causes, and that nature often brought about the cure; he followed sensible rules of fresh air and diet, which would help the work of nature in restoring the patient to health.[1]

Hippocrates seems to have been exactly what a physician should be—calm, full of wisdom and knowledge, caring greatly for his patients' welfare. He had many pupils and those that lived after him carried on his work in the same spirit.

When they began their work as doctors they took an oath (called the Hippocratic oath) that they would look on him who had taught them as a father, and would teach his sons without a fee; that they would hand on their knowledge to their sons, their master's sons, and their disciples, according to the law of physicians; that all their skill should be used for the good of the patient and that they should not talk about him to other people.

This oath (which is still taken by students at some medical schools) shows us what a high standard Hippocrates and his followers set for members of the great profession of medicine.

A Temple Cure.

In addition to ordinary medical treatment from the time of Hippocrates onwards, there were also what are called Temple Cures. We do not know when they began, but the one which we are about to describe probably did not flourish until the fifth century B.C. These cures lasted on into the time when Greece became part of the Roman Empire.

[1] The Greek word for nature is 'Phusis', from which we have the word 'physician'.

rest of the time was given up to athletic games, and also to musical contests, and the acting of plays. All of this was no doubt very good for the patients who were recovering, but we may imagine that those who were really ill were not sorry when the crowds of visitors departed and left them in peace.

XV

THE RISE OF MACEDON

GREECE IN THE FOURTH CENTURY B.C.

In Chapter XIII we left Athens under the power of Sparta, and in the next we shall see the whole of Greece obedient to the king of a country two hundred miles to the north. What happened during the sixty years between?

The Power of Persia.

In the Peloponnesian war certain Greek cities (particularly Sparta) called in the help of Persia, still a very great and rich power, and this went on with the result that Persia was able in 387 B.C. to force a treaty upon Greece. These are the words of the great king: 'King Artaxerxes thinks it just that the cities of Asia[1] shall belong to him. Further that all the other Greek cities, small and great, shall be free to govern themselves. If any refuse to accept this peace, I shall make war on them both by land and sea, with both ships and money.' This is called the King's Peace.

This peace was a disgrace to Greece, for it handed over

[1] The Greek cities on the western coast of what we now call Asia Minor and the islands near.

to Persia the cities of Asia Minor, which were truly Greek and had always kept in close touch with the homeland. As for the mainland states, it aimed in vain at preventing them from domineering over each other, and from forming leagues among themselves, but a Panhellenic (all-Greek) League against Persia, such as the orator Isocrates was always urging, never won their consent.

The City-States.

The struggles between city and city still went on. First Sparta won the leadership, and then (in 371 B.C.) Thebes became so strong under her great king Epaminondas that she defeated Sparta utterly at the battle of Leuctra in Boeotia. Nine years later Epaminondas was killed in battle and, with him, died the strength of Thebes.

Athens was now beginning to be again the leading state in Greece, but as the Greeks would never have combined under her or any other city, there would have been fresh wars and more exhaustion and weakness; the truth was that the day of the city-state was over and the day of larger powers had come. To the east lay one of these great powers, the old and dreaded enemy, Persia, while to the north was the growing kingdom of Macedonia, which soon became so strong that it could no longer be ignored; but before dealing with its history, we will return to Athens and see how the city and its citizens fared during this time.

Life at Athens during this century.

It is strange that in this troubled century life in Athens was a brilliant affair. Her ships sailed far and wide, and this traffic with other lands brought her not only riches, but fresh knowledge and new ideas. She became a centre of Greek thought and culture, and men came to her to study oratory (the art of public speaking) and philosophy.

Plato and Aristotle.

The greatest disciple of Socrates was Plato (427–347 B.C.), who not only wrote in polished and beautiful Greek an account of his master's life and teaching, but added much that was his own—his ideas of government and education, of man's mind and soul, of the nature of truth, goodness and beauty, and of the divine cause of all things. One of his

Fig. 33. A Greek in a himation   Fig. 34. A Greek woman in a peplos
(outer garment).   (outer garment).

best-known works is the *Republic*, in which he pictures an ideal state[1] framed and guided in accordance with his own philosophical views. Plato taught in the Academia, a gymnasium near Athens, adorned with shady trees and running waters, and his school is known as the Academy.

When Plato died his pupil, Aristotle, was already a well-

---

[1] Modern writers have written similar books of imagination, among which are Sir Thomas More's *Utopia* (from the Greek words for 'no place') and William Morris' *News from Nowhere*.

known philosopher. He taught in the shady walks of the Lyceum, a gymnasium on the outskirts of Athens. He sought eagerly after every kind of knowledge—science in all its branches, especially botany and zoology, ethics (the science of human conduct), logic (the science of reasoning), politics, and the art of poetry. All through the ages men have been influenced by these two great thinkers—Plato, who has been called 'the Father of Modern Philosophy', and Aristotle, 'the Father of Modern Science'.

There was not much building of temples in Athens now, but many new and beautiful statues were made. Often Greek artists went abroad and worked in foreign cities, thus spreading Greek culture and art.

The March of the Ten Thousand (401 B.C.).

In spite of all this brilliance, there was discontent, restlessness, and poverty in Athens and in other Greek cities, and many adventurous men left their cities and served as mercenaries (paid soldiers) of some foreign power. The most famous of these adventures was 'The March of the Ten Thousand' by a band of Greeks in the pay of a Persian prince called Cyrus who wanted to seize the Persian throne which had been held by Cyrus the Great 150 years before. Xenophon, a pupil of Socrates, tells us their experiences— a victorious battle near Babylon, the death of Cyrus, their own escape from treachery under Xenophon's leadership, and their retreat by unknown lands, across rivers, through deep snow, and mountain passes guarded by barbarous enemies. At last the men in front, reaching a mountain top, suddenly cried, 'The sea! The sea!' for they had reached the Black Sea and from there easily found their way home. This great adventure had shown them again that, as soldiers, they were better than the Persians.

MACEDON

The Macedonians.

The Macedonians looked on themselves as Greeks and spoke Greek, but the Greeks of the south called them barbarians and declared that they could not understand what they said. Probably they were partly Greek, but they had been far less civilized and polished than the pure Greeks. Archelaus, however, who was king from 413 to 399 B.C., wanted to introduce Greek civilization into his country and welcomed to his court Greek artists and poets, including Zeuxis, the great painter, and Euripides, the poet. One of his successors, Philip, was also a great admirer of Greek culture, and we shall see, in the following pages, how this affected the education and ideas of his son, Alexander.

Philip, king of Macedon (from 359 to 336 B.C.).

Philip had spent three years in Thebes and had learnt there how the Greeks formed their infantry in a close array called a phalanx. He adopted and developed this formation. His cavalry included a band of noble Macedonians known as his 'Companions', who, later, under Alexander, numbered two thousand, and with him attacked the enemy in battle. Philip was rich, for he had seized the gold mines of Thrace, and this wealth, together with the strength of his army, enabled him to threaten or make alliance with the Greek cities near him, and conquer or control the districts round the north and north-west of the Aegean. This growing power was like a heavy cloud overhanging Greece from the north, and the Athenians watched it, alarmed and distracted. Some of them agreed with Isocrates that the Greek states should combine, accept Philip as their leader and march against Persia; more, however, followed their most famous orator, Demosthenes, who attacked Philip in a number of speeches known as his *Philippics*.[1]

The advice of Demosthenes prevailed, and the Greeks prepared to oppose Philip, who marched into Greece, conquered Athens and Thebes in the battle of Chaeronea in Boeotia (338 B.C.), and thus made all the Greek states except Sparta acknowledge him as their leader. He then invited them to a great congress at Corinth where, calling himself their Leader, not their King, he told them of his plan to invade Persia at the head of his Macedonians and themselves. In 336 B.C. when he was about to set out, he was assassinated at the age of forty-six and his son, Alexander, reigned in his stead.

Alexander's Youth.

Among the tutors of Alexander was the famous philosopher Aristotle, whom Philip had invited to the court to educate him from the age of thirteen to sixteen. This was very important for, through Aristotle, Alexander became greatly interested in science, especially in medicine and nature study, and in Greek literature and ways. He is said to have slept with the Iliad (and a dagger) under his pillow, and he sent to Greece for copies of the great Greek tragedies when he was campaigning in Asia, years afterwards. But above all he admired the Iliad, and looked on Achilles, from whom his mother claimed descent, as his great hero. Alexander by no means lived only for study. When a boy he tamed a horse from Thessaly that Philip and his followers had been quite unable to manage; noticing that the horse shied and plunged at its own shadow, he calmed it, and after turning it towards the sun, he leapt on its back and let it go at full speed. This was the famous horse Bucephalus which he rode on his campaigns.

---

[1] A word afterwards used for a violent speech against anyone.

When Alexander was sixteen, Philip (being absent on war) put him in charge of the kingdom. During this time Alexander waged successfully a small war against a rebellious tribe, for he was already eager for conquest, and he feared that Philip would leave him nothing to conquer. At the battle of Chaeronea, he led the cavalry against the enemy. When he came to the throne at the age of twenty, men soon saw that a very great man was now entering into the world's history.

XVI

ALEXANDER THE GREAT

(King of Macedon from 336 to 323 B.C.)

Preparations against Persia.

Alexander spent the first two years after Philip's death in making his own frontiers safe, and bringing all the Greek states to accept him as their leader. He was then able, at the age of twenty-two, to start for the East in order to carry out Philip's plan of conquering Persia.

The king of Persia was Darius III, a handsome, imposing figure, but not to be compared with the great Darius of the first Persian war. His wealth was fabulous, his navy large and famous, his army enormous and unwieldy, and his empire stretched from Egypt and Asia Minor to India. Against this, Alexander had a comparatively small but well disciplined army, a small navy and a moderate income from his gold mines, pastures and forests; he had, however, courage and leadership and a firm belief in himself and his own destiny. Had not the prophetess at Delphi once said to him, 'My son, thou art invincible'?

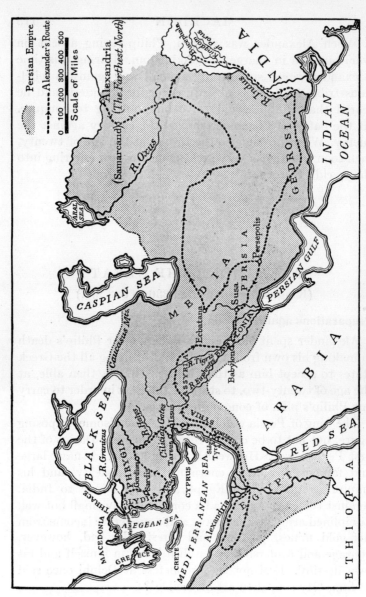

Map 11. The Persian empire and Alexander's route.

Asia Minor.

Alexander's first act, after crossing the Hellespont, was to go to Troy and there to lay a garland on the tomb of Achilles. He then marched on to the river Granicus, where he found the Persians posted on the opposite bank, prepared to stop his way with their spears and arrows. He charged across the river on his horse Bucephalus at the head of his Com-

Fig. 35. A Persian soldier.

panions, easily distinguished from the rest by his white-winged helmet. The Persians made him their mark, and one of them almost killed him with his scimitar, but his friend, Cleitus, struck it aside and saved his life. Then Alexander and his men put to flight the enemy that faced them, and by the onrush of his attack and the steady work of the phalanx the day was won. By this victory, followed by others, he was soon master of Asia Minor and had shut the ports against the Persian fleet.

Then, for his further advance eastwards, he gathered

his forces at Gordium in the central highlands of the country. Here there was the famous chariot of Gordius, an early king, the yoke of which was fastened by an intricate knot of cords, to be loosed—said the oracle—by him who would rule over Asia. Alexander, unable to untie it, cut the knot with his sword, and the thunder and lightning of the following night showed him that the oracle was fulfilled. (The phrase 'to cut the Gordian knot' is still used for solving a complicated difficulty in a direct and simple way.)

Alexander's route now lay through the Cilician gates (a pass in the mountains so narrow that it was said that 'a camel could not get through without unloading'). It was guarded by a garrison which fled at his approach, leaving the way open to Tarsus and thence towards Syria.

The Entry into Syria.

Meanwhile Darius was coming to stop his progress, and soon the two armies faced each other across a river in the plain of Issus (333 B.C.). Through the clever strategy of Alexander, the Persians were drawn up in a space much too narrow for their huge numbers, but still it was a hard struggle, and only when news came that Darius had fled, did the whole Persian army retreat. Their camp was seized, and the victorious army fell on the booty, but the tent and chariot of Darius were reserved for Alexander. 'Here,' says Plutarch, 'when he beheld the bathing vessels and the ointment boxes, all of gold curiously wrought, and smelt the fragrant odours with which the whole place was exquisitely perfumed, and thence passed into a pavilion of great size and height, where the couches and tables and preparations for an entertainment were perfectly magnificent, he turned to those about him and said, "This, it seems, is royalty."' He heard wailing in an adjoining tent and, on hearing that it came from the mother, wife and two daughters of the king, he sent a message telling them that Darius was still alive and that they themselves were in no danger.

Alexander did not follow Darius in his eastward flight, but marched south into Syria and down the coast to Tyre, a strong naval base built on an island half a mile from the coast. He laid siege to it, and after seven months of desperate resistance, he took it by storm.

Egypt.

When he had conquered Syria and Palestine, he entered Egypt, which was also part of the Persian dominions. It submitted to him, and proclaimed him Pharaoh (the title of all Egyptian kings). On one of his journeys in this country he passed through a fishing village on the delta of the Nile, and here, seeing how splendidly it was situated for trade and intercourse, he founded a Greek city called Alexandria, one of the many cities to which he gave this name, but far surpassing all the rest.

West of the Nile were the famous temple and oracle of the Egyptian god, Ammon. After a journey of eight or nine days into the desert, Alexander came to an oasis of one or two square miles, with wells, springs, palms and olives. Here was the oracle, and here he was received by the priests as the son of the god, for all Pharaohs were looked on as divine. He revealed to no one what he was told at the shrine, only that he had 'heard what was to his mind'. The welcome of the priests and the utterance of the oracle seem to have echoed his own feeling that he had power and a future beyond those of ordinary men; he had broken the domination of Persia round the Mediterranean, and he now set himself to conquer her empire to its farthest limits.

The heart of the Empire.

Alexander marched eastward across the Euphrates to the Tigris, where he conquered Darius in the battle of Gaugamela

(331 B.C.), a village near Arbela. Darius fled, and Alexander
entered his capitals, Babylon and Susa, which admitted
him, and Persepolis, which he took by storm. The amazing
wealth of these imperial cities was now his—nearly 180,000
talents of gold and silver, coined and uncoined, and quantities
of purple dye and other treasures. 'The spoils from Persepolis', said Plutarch, 'were so great that twenty thousand
mules and five thousand camels could hardly have carried
them.' He pursued Darius, and overtook him in the district
south of the Caspian Sea, only to find that he had been
fatally wounded by one of his own satraps, and his fellow
conspirators. Alexander gave Darius a royal burial, and
from this time he looked on himself as king of Persia.

So far, his army had followed him willingly. He shared
their dangers and toils, he cared for their welfare; he gave
them rewards, games, festivities, and rest between the
marches and battles; but now a great scheme was forming
in his mind, which they could not understand.

He loved and admired Greek culture—its language,
literature and art—and all the knowledge of it with which
Aristotle had inspired him in his boyhood—and he wanted
to spread this culture everywhere. He saw, too, that the
Persians could not be classed as mere barbarians, and he
wanted to join together Persians and Greeks, including
the best things in both nations, in one wide dominion with
himself as king. He filled the gaps in his army with Persians,
and he gave their nobles a share in the rule of the conquered provinces; this displeased many of his followers
and the first murmurs of discontent arose. His men had
had ample plunder; they were tired of war, and they wanted
to return to their homes which they had left four years
before. They disliked the favours shown to Persians, their
oriental ways, their prostration before the king—as to a
god—and the gorgeous Persian robes in which he received

them. The men were discontented, and even some of Alexander's best friends were suspected of rebellion, for which they were put to death. The battles and marches, the endless organization, the founding of cities, the effect of his own wounds—all this was a great strain on him, which showed itself later in a moment of passion. At a banquet at which both had drunk freely, he killed his great friend Cleitus, in anger at some scoffing words, and never afterwards forgave himself.

The Far East and the Return.

Alexander crossed the snowy Hindu Kush mountains into the upper valley of the Indus. From his adventures there, we will take only one example, his battle with Porus, king of part of the modern Punjab. Plutarch tells us that he was nearly seven feet high, and that when he rode on his huge elephant 'he appeared to be proportionately mounted, as a horseman on his horse'. With great difficulty Alexander overcame him in a hard-fought battle. When Porus was taken prisoner, and Alexander asked him how he wished to be treated, he replied, 'As a king', and though his country was now to become part of the Macedonian dominions, Alexander made him king over it and even gave him wider lands to rule than before.

Soon after this Alexander's famous steed, Bucephalus, died and he founded in his memory a city called Bucephala close to the scene of his battle on the Indus.

The country beyond this was only dimly known. Alexander had no idea that India stretched to the south and Asia far to the east. He longed to explore as far as the Ganges to see if its waters flowed into the ocean which encircled the earth; he wanted to find out about the mines, the plants, the animals, and to open up trade routes, as well as to conquer.

At this point his men refused to follow him any farther. The last fight against Porus had taken the edge off their courage; they heard that the distant Ganges was four miles wide and six hundred feet deep, and that the opposite bank was crowded with troops to say nothing of six thousand elephants. In eight years they had marched nearly twelve hundred miles. Not one step farther would they go. Alexander was obliged to give way and gave orders for the retreat; he himself with his own troops went a long way round, exploring to the mouth of the Indus and thence across the Gedrosian desert. At last all the forces met at Babylon; but here, suddenly, Alexander contracted a fever and after twelve days' illness he died, in the summer of 323 B.C., at the age of thirty-two.

The Greek historian, Arrian, gives an account of his last days showing how much he was still admired and loved:

On the sixth day of his fever, he was very seriously ill and was carried into the palace; he could still recognize his officers, but he could not speak. That night he was in high fever, and the day following and the next night, and the next day. His soldiers longed to see him; some that they might behold him while he was yet alive; others because it was announced that he was already dead, and they thought that his death was being hushed up by the bodyguard; most of them, because of their grief and longing for him, forced their way into his presence. They saw that he was speechless, but, as they filed past, he greeted them one by one by just raising his head and signing to them with his eyes.

The next evening he died. One of his generals, to whom he had given his signet ring, took over the command and the army returned to Greece.

What are we to make of Alexander and his amazing achievements? The Greeks had a favourite maxim, 'Nothing in excess', and in their eyes, he was too extreme and immoderate, a defect which grew on him in his later conquests.

Yet none could deny his love of Greek culture, and his extraordinary power, which might have been used for uniting the whole Greek world in the bonds of peace. In his days, however, war was taken for granted, and his thought naturally turned to it. He was not merely a commander of genius, but he had a mind which surpassed that of other men in power and grasp, together with the vigour and force to carry his far-reaching plans into effect. He may justly be called 'The Great', not only because he was one of the greatest generals of history, but because he spread Greek culture and ideas over the Eastern world.

XVII

THE HELLENISTIC AGE

Alexander had left no heir, and for forty years his generals and their successors warred among themselves in their efforts to become princes of the districts left in their charge. A number of monarchies arose, the most important and lasting of which were Egypt, Syria and Macedonia. The Far East, in time, came under rulers of its own. The Greek cities remained under Macedonian rule but with considerable freedom; Athens, though her glorious days were over, was still a centre of culture; and the wars between the cities still went on. We are inclined to ask, 'What difference did Alexander, after all, make to the world?' The answer is, 'All the difference; the world was never the same again.'

We shall see this if we look at the next two hundred years. It is called the Hellenistic period, because of the wonderful way in which the ideas of greater Greece—of all Hellas— now influenced the world.

Fig. 36. Courtyard of a house of this period (reconstruction).

ALEXANDRIA, AND THE ARTS AND SCIENCES

The City.

Egypt was ruled by a line of kings called Ptolemy, the name
of one of Alexander's generals who became ruler of the
country. Mariners sailing towards the city, but still—it is
said—thirty miles away, could see before them a light
shining in the distance. This was from the famous lighthouse,
four hundred feet high or more, on the island of Pharos[1]
north of the city of Alexandria, which had been founded by
Alexander when he visited Egypt. The lighthouse was one
of the seven wonders of the ancient world.

Like all Greek cities of the age, Alexandria was well designed,
with parallel and intersecting streets, and fine buildings.

[1] The French word for lighthouse is 'un phare'.

The city was built on a belt of sand between the Mediterranean and a large lake. Into its harbours came ships and traders of all nations, and produce from the whole world, including gold from Spain, and tin from Cornwall and Brittany. The outgoing ships carried, among other things, corn, linen and paper. Corn first, for neither Greece nor Rome ever grew enough for its own needs, and Alexandria, with its bountiful supplies from the Nile valley, was one of

Fig. 37. The lighthouse of Alexandria (reconstruction).

the great corn marts of the world. Linen was also a famous product of Egypt, and we know its quality from the wrappings of linen round the mummies in our museums, still fresh and strong, though it was woven more than two thousand years ago. 'Paper', another gift of the Nile, was made from the papyrus, a tall reed which grew in Egypt; its fibres, cut into strips, were stuck together side by side, and thus formed a surface for writing. Lengths of this were made, and could be rolled up when not in use. (Our word 'paper' comes from 'papyrus', though ours is no longer made from reeds.)

All this commerce was helped by two things. One was the enormous amount of gold which Alexander's army had brought back from Persia and India, and which was now current, coined and uncoined, in the known world; the other was the use everywhere of the Greek language.

As we have seen, this had been Alexander's aim and ideal, and now it had actually happened. Greeks of all ranks,

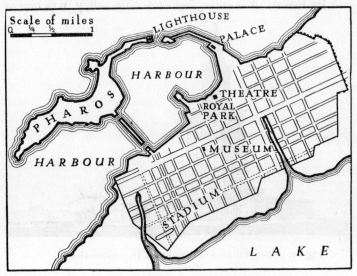

Map 12. Plan of Alexandria.

fired with the spirit of adventure or driven by need, were scattered everywhere, and Greek had become a universal language (like Latin in the Middle Ages) spoken in all the towns, though in the countryside many of the natives could speak only in their own tongue.

Alexandria was the most magnificent of all the cities which were modelled after the Greek pattern. On the sea front was the Royal Palace, and, at a short distance, the

Museum (home of the Muses, daughters of Zeus, protecting the arts and sciences). This was not a building stocked with things of the past, but was a gathering-place—almost a university—for learned men from all parts of the Greek world who gave up their lives to study, and were helped by money from the king and by his great library of 20,000 papyrus rolls—the first public library, as it has been called.

Geography.

Alexander is said to have left the known world four times greater than he found it, and it was at Alexandria that the science of geography, as we know it, began. A scholar called Eratosthenes calculated the circumference of the earth (he made it one-seventh too large) and drew a map with eight lines of latitude and seven of longitude—a great advance in geography. The map given below shows us the world as imagined by Eratosthenes, and is based on the geographical knowledge of his day. You will notice that the northern coast of Europe is drawn vaguely, with queerly-shaped islands, Britain and Ireland, to the north of it. The Nile has its right direction and also the Indus, but there is a strange mistake about the Caspian Sea, which is con-nected with the Arctic Ocean, and there is a stunted shallow look about Africa and India.

Scientific Discovery.

Alexander's journeys had let loose a flood of new know-ledge, for all through his campaigns he had been accompanied by scientists who studied and recorded anything of interest. After his death, there was so much movement in the Greek world that scholars everywhere could get into touch with one another, and they made discovery after discovery with the eagerness and spirit of enquiry that were characteristic of the Greek mind. We must not forget that science in all

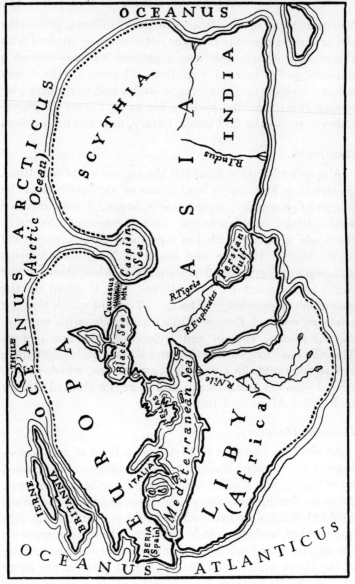

Map 13. The world according to Eratosthenes.

OCEANUS

OCEANUS ARCTICUS (Arctic Ocean)

SCYTHIA

ASIA

INDIA

R.Indus

Caspian Sea

Persian Gulf

Caucasus Mt.

R.Tigris

R.Euphrates

R.Nile

Black Sea

THULE

OCEANUS

EUROPA

IERNE

BRITANNIA

ITALIA

Mediterranean Sea

IBERIA (Spain)

LIBYA (Africa)

OCEANUS ATLANTICUS

its branches owes an immense debt to Alexander's tutor, Aristotle. He was a great reader himself, and with the help of his students he searched carefully into the progress of the various sciences up to his own time, and made a record of it in books. His own chief sciences were botany and zoology, and, to help his work, he not only observed plants and animals himself, but he questioned all sorts of outdoor people, such as fishermen, cattle-breeders and huntsmen, to find out what they had noticed. From this mass of information he was able to divide plants and animals into classes, and to work up gradually from his observation of single cases to general laws of nature. His work was of the greatest possible value to Alexandrian scientists.

Mathematical Advance.

A famous scholar of Alexandria called Euclid, who flourished about 300 B.C., using and adding to the mathematical knowledge which had been growing for many years, wrote his *Elements of Geometry*, which was used as a textbook everywhere until the end of the nineteenth century A.D.; it has been said that no book in the world except the Bible has had such a reign. King Ptolemy showed great interest in the *Elements*, but found them hard. 'Is there no easier way of learning geometry', he asked, 'than by ploughing through your Elements?' 'Sire,' was the answer, 'to geometry there is no royal road.'

In 287 B.C. there was born at Syracuse a mathematician of genius and the founder of the science of mechanics, whose name was Archimedes. We will take only two of his discoveries. First, the use of levers, by which a small force can move a great weight. A huge ship of over 4000 tons had been built at Syracuse but could not be launched. 'Give me a place to stand,' said Archimedes, when asked for his help, 'and I will move the world.' He then applied to the difficulty his system of leverage, and launched the ship by means of toothed wheels and an endless screw, or by the pulley which he is said to have invented. Another dramatic use of this device is told in Chapter VIII of Part II ('The Romans').

Here is the story of another of his discoveries as told by Vitruvius, a Roman writer on architecture.

The king of Syracuse, having vowed a golden crown to the gods, ordered it to be made from a piece of gold carefully weighed beforehand. The contractor made a crown of the right weight, but was afterwards suspected of having stolen some of the gold, mixing in silver in its stead. The king asked Archimedes to help him to detect the theft. But how? While Archimedes was pondering about this he happened to go to the bath and noticed that the more he covered his body with water, the more water ran over the top. He leapt out, full of joy, and, naked as he was, rushed home crying, 'Eureka! Eureka!' (I have found it. I have found it.) He made a mass of silver and a mass of gold of the same weight as the crown, and then filled a large vessel with water. First he lowered in the silver; the overflow of water corresponded with its volume. He took out the silver, refilled the jar and lowered in the gold, and found that much less water was displaced because the volume of the gold was less than the volume of the silver. Lastly he filled the vessel again and lowered in the crown; he found that more water was displaced than would have been the case with a crown of the same weight made entirely of gold. He thus showed that the crown was not of pure gold. Archimedes next made other blocks containing gold mixed with various proportions of silver, but always of the same weight as the crown. Finally he obtained a block which displaced exactly as much water as the crown. The king knew then how much gold had been taken.

Mathematics and the various branches of mechanics (hydrostatics for example) went a long way beyond what can be described in this book. The science of astronomy was aided by mathematics including trigonometry, and wonderful discoveries were made. Aristarchus made calculations as to the relative distance of the sun and the moon from the earth, and suggested that the earth and other planets revolved round the sun. Plutarch was shocked at this denial that the earth was the centre of the solar system, and the same disapproval was shown when Galileo, followed by Copernicus, rediscovered the same thing hundreds of years later. Other astronomers calculated the position of the most important stars.

Development of Medicine.

We saw in Chapter xiv what a splendid start in medical science was made by Hippocrates. In the Hellenistic age his ideas were carried on and much progress was made in the knowledge of the working of the brain, the nervous system and the heart. Anatomy was studied and practised, surgery advanced, and among all this learning and research, common sense was not forgotten, and doctors again and again taught the need of sensible food and plenty of gymnastics.

Literature.

There were many literary men at Alexandria who studied the masterpieces of the past, and these men not only saved for us a large number of manuscripts of Greek works, but also showed how such writings should be judged and edited. Our knowledge of the Classics owes a great debt to Alexandria.

Some of the prose and verse written in this age was learned and artificial, but there was one poet, Theocritus, who wrote charming poems which he called idylls (little pictures) of daily life, such as that of shepherds tending their flocks, and singing laments when one of their number had died. The Roman poet, Virgil, modelled some of his poems on this pastoral poetry as it is called. His shepherds often stand for friends of his own day, and our own poet, Milton, used the same idea when he wanted to write a lament in memory of his friend, the young poet, Edward King, who had been drowned at sea. He called him 'Lycidas', after one of the names used by Theocritus, and wrote this lament as if he too were a shepherd bewailing a lost friend in the pastures of the countryside.

Perhaps the most important piece of literary work was the translation of the Old Testament into Greek by order of King Ptolemy II of Egypt. By this time the Jews were scattered over the whole civilized world, mainly in cities which were the centres of commerce. They no longer spoke Hebrew, the language in which the Old Testament had been written, but used instead a form of it called Aramaic. For general use, however, in the districts dwelt in by the Jews, Greek was the best-known language, and this translation of the Old Testament into Greek was not only a great boon for the Jews but for the whole world. Men had for a long time been groping after the idea of one God, and, as the Jews had always made this the centre of their religious thought, it was a gift to the world that their holy writings should now come into the hands of all thinkers, in a language which they could understand.

The translation is called the Septuagint, from the old Jewish legend that it was translated by seventy scholars (Latin: 'Septuaginta', seventy) in the same words, though they had not seen each other's versions. We now know that the translation of the Hebrew scriptures covered many years and was perhaps not finished much before the birth

The Fifth Century

B.C.	(a)	(b)
499–493	Ionian revolt against Persia	
490	Battle of Marathon	
		484 Prize for Tragedy won by Aeschylus for the first time
480	Battles of Thermopylae and Salamis Carthaginian forces annihilated by Greeks at Himera in Sicily	480 Birth of Herodotus (historian of the Persian Wars)
478	Confederacy of Delos Leadership of Pericles at Athens The Athenian Empire	
		468 Prize for Tragedy won by Sophocles for the first time
		c. 460 Birth of Hippocrates (father of Greek Medicine)
457	Building of the Long Walls begun	
447–438	Building of the Parthenon	
431	Outbreak of the Peloponnesian War	From 431 B.C. Production of many plays by Euripides and Aristophanes
	430 The Plague	
	429 Death of Pericles	
	425 Capture of Sphacteria	
	421 Peace of Nicias	
	415 Sicilian Expedition	Thucydides, historian of the Peloponnesian War up to 411 B.C. (about 460–400 B.C.)
	405 Battle of Aegospotami	
404	The Fall of the Athenian Empire	
403	Democracy restored at Athens Power of Sparta	
		399 Death of Socrates
		427–347 Plato

The Fourth Century

371–362	Period of Theban leadership	

The Rise of Macedon

359–336	Philip, King of Macedon	
		351 Demosthenes' First Speech against Philip
		343 Aristotle (philosopher) becomes tutor to Alexander
336–323	Alexander, King of Macedon	
	331 Foundation of Alexandria	

The Hellenistic Age

B.C.	(a)	(b)
About 300 B.C.	Break-up of Alexander's Empire, leading to rise of separate monarchies, the most important being Egypt, Macedonia, Syria	321 Menander's first play *c.* 300 Euclid (mathematician) flourished 287–212 Archimedes (mathematician and physicist) *c.* 250 Eratosthenes (geographer) flourished *c.* 270 Theocritus flourished

INDEX

Note on the usual English pronunciation of proper names

1. Vowels are marked – (long); ◡ (short); ⌒ (where two vowels combine to form a diphthong).

E.g. Dē′los (pronounced Dee̅′-los); Phĭ′lip (pronounced as in English); Croê′sus (pronounced Krē′-sus).

Emphasis is laid on the syllables marked ′.

2. *Vowel sounds* (including diphthongs) are pronounced as in English:

ae is usually pronounced ē, e.g. Daê′dalus

ei	,,	,,	ī ,, Cleî′tus
oe	,,	,,	ē ,, Croê′sus
eu	,,	,,	ū ,, Euclid.

3. *Consonants:*

c before e, i or y is pronounced like s, e.g. Ci′rce (pronounced Si′rsē).

ch is pronounced like k, e.g. Achi′lles (pronounced A-ki′ll-ēs), Charybd′is (pronounced Karibd′is).

g before e or i is pronounced like j, e.g. Aêgē′an (pronounced Ē-jē′-an).

Note:

(1) All syllables are sounded, e.g. Alcibi′ades (five syllables).

(2) The usual English pronunciation is shown in square brackets against names which differ from the Greek pronunciation in length of vowel.

(3) Guidance is given in round brackets for a few words which might present difficulties.

INDEX

INDEX

CHART SHOWING THE OVERLAPPING OF GREEK AND ROMAN HISTORY, 800–1 B.C.

	GREECE	ROME
800–700 B.C.	Growth of the City-States 776 B.C. The first Olympic Games THE GREAT PERIOD	753 B.C. Founding of Rome *Rome governed by kings*
700–600 B.C.	OF GREEK COLONIZATION	
600–500 B.C.	In this century the *Ionian cities* of Asia Minor were in a high state of culture; the constitution of *Sparta* was fixed (about 600 B.C.) and the constitution of *Athens* went through various changes leading to *Democracy*	Etruscan power at its height Driving out of the kings

500–400 B.C.	First Persian invasion (Marathon)
	Second Persian invasion (Salamis)
	Confederacy of Delos
	Age of Pericles. Athens becomes an Empire
	Peloponnesian War
	    ,,
	    ,, Defeat of Athens Socrates
		THE REPUBLIC
		Tribunes for the Plebeians instituted
		
		Beginning of Rome's conquest of Italy
		The Decemviri and the Twelve Tables (of law)